Intentional Wealth

Intentional Wealth

How Families Build Legacies of Stewardship and Financial Health

Courtney Pullen

TABLE OF CONTENTS

ENDORSEMENTS

Too many conversations among affluent families begin and end around the money. Courtney Pullen shares a pathway, proven by the successful families he has served, which will transform the way you think and talk about stewardship and financial well-being. Intentional Wealth will inspire all who read it to purposefully create a positive and sustainable legacy.

John A. Warnick, Founder
Purposeful Planning Institute

Courtney Pullen's new book, Intentional Wealth, helps families and their advisors understand the concept of stewardship as an intentional set of practices that help a family flourish. The intention to avoid the "shirt sleeves to shirt sleeves" outcome that is all too often the fate of a family, and the practice of stewardship toward bringing to life the dreams of all family members as the means of doing so, is Courtney's gift to all families. We are blessed to have this gift.

James (Jay) E. Hughes, Jr.
author of *Family Wealth—Keeping It in the Family*
and *Family: The Compact Among Generations*
and co-author of *The Cycle of the Gift*

Courtney has done a wonderful job in providing a thoughtful, practical guide to help families understand how financial wealth can be used to fully benefit multiple generations. He blends decades of experience, common sense, and academic knowledge to provide a complete picture of the challenges and the opportunities. Every family should read this honest book.

Katherine Lintz, CEO and Founder
Matter Family Office

The impact of the body of work presented in Intentional Wealth will eventually be a measurable increase in the number of legacy families and their contributions to the overall good of humanity. Courtney Pullen does not waste time searching for magic formulas, he gives us the Ten Habits of Healthy Families as the essential components families and their advisors can use to construct their own path to multi-generational well-being. This is the guidebook families of wealth have been looking for. It is a wonderful combination of old truths and fresh thinking laid out in clear steps supported by meaningful stories.

Susan Bradley CFP®, Founder
Sudden Money Institute®
Institute for Certified Financial Transitionist®

To families everywhere who are investing in the
future of their family and its members.

To my family—Mimi, McKenna, Conner, Katie, Emily, and
Sam—who continue to teach me the meaning of family.

ACKNOWLEDGEMENTS

To my friends and collaborators, with appreciation for their commitment to working with families and helping the world along the way:

Collaboration for Flourishing Families (CFF)
thelearningspacedc.com

The Purposeful Planning Institute
purposefulplanninginstitute.com

Connect-Gens
www.connect-gens.com

The Leadership Council
Thriving families—Thriving world.

Editor and collaborator extraordinaire, Kathleen Fox

INTRODUCTION

"FROM SHIRT SLEEVES to shirt sleeves in three generations."
This is an ancient saying about the fleeting nature of wealth, and
modern research has confirmed its accuracy. Approximately 90%
of affluent families lose their wealth by the end of the third generation. The tragedy of this statistic isn't the loss of the money;
it's the loss of the family that goes with it. As the wealth dissi-
pates, so does the connective tissue of the family, whose members often end up disconnected and embroiled in conflict. To me,
this is unacceptable. It is tragic not only for these families, but for
the communities they live in and for our culture.

The crucial question that this book attempts to answer is:
What are the other 10% doing? There are wealthy families that
flourish. They are successful, not just in maintaining inherited
wealth, but in passing on intentional legacies of stewardship
and values. I have devoted my career to understanding what
these thriving families do and to helping other families learn
from them. My work is to help families go from shirt sleeves to
success.

This book describes the strategies used by wealthy families
who manage their wealth intentionally and successfully create
family missions of stewardship and legacies of balance and well-
being. It provides tools for any family, regardless of its net worth,
that wishes to do the same. These tools are valuable for all families wanting to build lasting patterns of financial and emotional
health on a foundation of integrity and responsibility. I use these
strategies to help families who are doing well and want to do

better. I also use them to help struggling families restore themselves to health.

The typical profile of a wealthy family looks something like this: Generation One is entrepreneurial—the individual, couple, or siblings whose inventiveness, hard work, risk-taking, and success create the initial wealth. Generation Two tends to maintain the wealth while holding to the original values. Generation Three tends to consume and even squander the wealth.

In addition, every family has quirks, patterns, and tolerances that have developed over decades. Wealth exacerbates a family's preexisting fault lines. The generational time clock converts minor annoyances into brick walls of disunity. For wealthy families, it is essential to think in terms of several generations. Building healthy, productive families requires considering the needs of individual family members, the internal harmony of the family, and the impact outside of the family system and into the future.

For many families of significant means, money was the outcome, not the goal, of the generation that created the wealth. The focus of the original wealth creator was to build a business, invent a process, or develop and use a talent. Getting rich was more of a career by-product than a life goal. This person or family, then, didn't necessarily learn the skills for managing wealth, much less the skills for passing that wealth forward in healthy ways.

Over the years I have worked with many families who want to build stronger family systems and transfer wealth to succeeding generations in constructive rather than destructive ways. They face the ongoing challenge of passing on, not only the family money, but also the values that brought that wealth to the family in the first place. These families understand that wealth, just like other life-defining circumstances such as poverty, serious illness, tragedy, or fame, carries its own blessings and its own burdens.

The needs and challenges of a family with a net worth of

billions differ from those of a family worth 200 million dollars, one worth 20 or 30 million dollars, or one with a net worth of one or two million dollars. Still, every family I've worked with or interviewed has faced the following dilemma: How do we achieve success that includes financial prosperity, enjoy the fruits of that success, and yet pass on to our children and grandchildren a legacy of financial and emotional health? How do we create a family mission of stewardship and freedom, rather than one of dysfunction and self-indulgence? How do we help family members build empowered relationships with money?

Certainly, these concerns are not unique to the rich or even to modern society. The perception that younger generations "have it easier than we did" and "don't appreciate what they have" is a cliché that has been around for centuries. It might be argued, however, that today's world increasingly celebrates conspicuous consumption and fosters a sense of entitlement. In addition, what we now consider an upper-middle-class lifestyle increasingly includes elements of luxury and convenience that once were reserved for the rich.

Many families who don't live lavishly and wouldn't consider themselves rich also may create more wealth than they realize. Small business owners, farmers and ranchers who may be income poor but land rich, or couples who both have high-earning professional careers can easily retire with a net worth of several million dollars. That is more than enough to lead to concern about the legacy they want to leave to their children and grandchildren.

There is one unique aspect of great wealth, however, that can foster dysfunction: the lack of a need to say "no." This power to do anything, unrestricted by lack of money, lack of access, or people in one's life with the authority and courage to say "no," can be as corrupting as any other kind of unlimited power. The challenge for wealthy families is to create a family environment which employs that power in ways to foster emotional, physical, and financial health.

Many families are meeting that challenge with intentionality, integrity, and success. Over the past 15 years I have been privileged to work with some of them.

For close to 30 years I have been in the business of helping people. First I worked as a psychotherapist, then as a consultant for management, corporations, and family businesses. For the past 15 years I have specialized in working with affluent families. I remember distinctly the first family I worked with. I had been an advisor to a financial services firm and they described their concerns about their largest client. This was a prominent family that had been financially successful and who were embroiled in conflict. They asked me to meet with the family and see if I could help. That experience was so profound and so successful that it led me to change the focus of my career.

Among the many things I have learned in working with families is the importance of paying attention to what works. What can we learn from the 10% of the families that are being successful? How can we reach more families and increase that percentage of successful families to 20% or more?

This book is based on interviews with families that are making it. I interviewed family members who were well into the third generation from the original wealth creator and very consciously working as a family on flourishing. I interviewed family members who had made it to the fourth, fifth, and sixth generations. I also interviewed professionals such as estate attorneys and wealth advisors who were working with families that were flourishing. Several of the families mentioned in this book I have worked with. All of the names and stories have been changed to protect their confidentiality.

Most of the families I met were quite humble. They didn't want to be looked up to as a family that "had made it." One in particular said, "We are just doing more things right than wrong." Many described heartaches and challenges, and they were unwavering in their commitment that their family was worth the investment of time and energy.

Family is a paradox for many of us. Our children are our greatest source of pride and joy and our greatest challenge. We worry: "Will they be okay?" This book is written particularly for families being faced with the unique challenges of wealth. While most of the concepts and stories apply to all families, I talk specifically about what is difficult about growing up rich.

Many of my findings were initially a surprise because they weren't found in the research. As I look back, however, they reflected common sense. One of the most important elements for thriving families was summed up by a number of business owners who said something like the following:

"I need to bring as much attention to my family as I did to my business. I didn't run my business on making it up as I went. My success was grounded in sound business principles and being clear about mission, vision, and strategy. I need to bring the same intention to my family."

The stories that follow are about families who brought that level of intention to making their families successful. This success was not defined by more money but by a richer family.

Essentially, the questions I asked were: "What makes a good family, one that is successful for generations and flourishes? What does it take to create a healthy family culture?" Again, many of the ideas offered by thriving families weren't radical. Their success wasn't because of a superior financial investment strategy, but because of investing in healthy communication based on trust. This may seem like common sense, but unfortunately it isn't common practice for many families.

Intentional Wealth is about what works. It describes what you can do. Keep in mind that change occurs in the direction of your attention. As you learn more about what works, you can create more of that for you and your family.

Families who manage their wealth with attention and intention help individual family members create empowered relationships with money. They model and sustain what it means to lead a rich life—a life enhanced yet not dominated by material wealth.

CHAPTER ONE

FROM ENTITLEMENT TO EMPOWERMENT

"I deserve it, and I should have it."
"I should always get everything I want."
"My needs and wants should always come first."
"There's no reason not to do or have anything I want."
"It's mine, and don't you dare try to take it away from me!"

BELIEFS SUCH AS these are typical of a sense of entitlement. It may be perfectly normal for the average toddler to feel entitled, but no parent sets out to raise a child who still feels this way as an adult. Why is an attitude of entitlement so common in affluent families?

Part of the problem may be that a sense of entitlement seems to be a normal condition for human beings. No matter what comforts, indulgences, or rewards we get, or whatever lifestyle we become accustomed to, it doesn't take long for us to start assuming we're entitled to that lifestyle and have a right to keep it. This is true whether we're talking about children's allowances, Social Security checks, employee benefits like health insurance, or clean water and plowed streets. It also, of course, applies to the privileges and power that come with wealth.

Most of us, as children, come up against barriers, setbacks, and unpleasant realities that challenge our sense of entitlement. Parents, teachers, and even our peers insist we learn to share our toys and wait our turns. They make us learn to take care of ourselves and help with household chores instead of being waited on like the little despots we would prefer to be. They limit our allowances, say no to buying us ponies or cars or expensive designer jeans, and in all sorts of ways let us know that we can't do and have whatever we want whenever we want it.

As we grow up, the world around us imposes its own limits. We learn that we can't have upper-middle-class lifestyles on entry-level salaries. We learn—sometimes through painful consequences—that it's a good idea to follow society's rules about everything from speed limits to professional dress codes. We figure out that our lives are more comfortable if we compromise and get along with fellow employees and friends who won't always let us be in charge. These limits teach us that, just because we may feel we deserve something, it doesn't mean we automatically can or should have it right this minute.

Money Dissolves Many Limits

For children from wealthy families, many of these inherent barriers and setbacks do not exist. There is rarely any need for parents to say "no" for financial reasons. On the contrary, there may be family members who go out of their way to provide experiences and possessions that kids haven't even thought of wanting.

Money also has the power to dissolve many of society's limits. The ability to buy one's way out of trouble can mitigate the pain of both mistakes in judgment and deliberate rule-breaking. This interference with natural consequences can prevent both children and adults from learning to take responsibility for their actions.

Growing up in a wealthy family can result in a sense of surrealism, where the exotic becomes commonplace. As one young man said about skiing, "I heli-ski because I can." There was no need for him to consider whether he could afford to hire a helicopter to drop him off on top of a mountain. He didn't need to choose between heli-skiing and another winter sport, or to save money for a special heli-skiing vacation. He didn't necessarily even have to like heli-skiing all that much. It was just another activity that his family could easily afford and easily arrange to do.

People who are wealthy have the option of starting every day with an open appointment book. There are no outside restrictions on their activities. They have the time, money, and power to choose to do exactly what they want. Certainly, many wealthy people work hard and spend their days productively: managing businesses, caring for families, overseeing foundations, and contributing to their communities. Yet they aren't required to work hard in order to make their mortgage payments and put food on the table. They always have the choice of walking away and doing whatever they feel like doing, whether it is for their own good or their own harm.

In a wealthy family, there is no need to say no on financial grounds. If parents deny their children a lavish birthday party, a stay at summer camp, a redecorated bedroom, or a pony, the kids know perfectly well that the refusal isn't because the family can't afford it. It isn't easy to be the hard-hearted parent who deprives a child simply out of choice. Parents unable to fall back on "we can't afford it" may find it hard to justify saying no. It doesn't necessarily occur to them that "no" is a complete sentence and sometimes no justification is needed.

One wealthy family consulted me because members of the second generation were having difficulty living within their means. The wealth creator had made significant money and invested it wisely. The second generation all began to live quite lavish lifestyles, and the first generation was concerned about the message being sent to their grandchildren.

A member of the second generation said he was embarrassed

to have trouble living on his more-than-ample income. When he was growing up and the family was still in the middle class, living within their means was easy. As he put it, "You only had so much money and you didn't spend more than you made. The limits were exceedingly clear. But now it's like there are no clear rules or limits. It's hard to emotionally make sense of significant wealth. The rules that applied for me growing up no longer apply and it feels like I have no bumpers on my life."

Another family followed a path of entitlement that is, unfortunately, not uncommon. The father had made millions in a high-profile law practice, being so focused on his career that he rarely spent time with his three children as they were growing up. As each one turned 21, he put two million dollars into an account for them. He put no restrictions on their use of the money, nor had he and his wife done anything to teach the children how to manage their wealth.

The oldest son started a business that, thanks to several costly mistakes, ate up his two million in a hurry. The younger son slipped into a "playboy" lifestyle of partying, drug abuse, and self-destructive drama. The daughter announced her disdain for the wealthy and gave most of her money away to struggling artists, aspiring musicians, and a variety of causes.

The oldest son, after some difficult times, did eventually begin to learn from his mistakes and make a success of his business. The younger son and the daughter didn't do as well, experimenting with one career choice after another and bouncing from one financial crisis to another. All three of them kept coming back to Dad for more money, seeming to regard him as a convenient ATM with a high withdrawal limit. And Dad, feeling guilty over his own mistakes and lack of involvement in their lives, kept giving it to them.

Money Can Insulate Us from Natural Consequences

Having a significant sum of money can often separate someone from the natural consequences of life. These consequences include the feedback from other people that is an important factor in learning appropriate social behavior.

Psychologists say our sense of self is formed through mirroring from our primary caretakers. When a baby smiles or makes a cooing sound, what are we compelled to do but smile and coo back? That form of mirroring, over time, gives the baby a sense of self. When a three-year-old shows her parents her art, which in reality is just a bunch of scribbles, the parents ooh and aah over the beautiful pictures, recognizing the child's creativity and greatness as a human being. When that same child shows us her art as a third grader, our response is less demonstrative, as we intuitively know we need to mirror back in an age-appropriate manner.

This mirroring process is also how parents shape children's experiences to a degree. If a child does something the parents deem inappropriate, just a look of disapproval, a raised voice, or even the lack of a favorable response gives the child the feedback that this behavior is not acceptable. This mirroring and shaping process is fundamental for the early years of a child's life.

As children get older, their friends and peers begin to influence them as much as or more than their parents. Their lives become more socially constructed. To a large degree, growing children view themselves in the manner that the people around them view them. This was demonstrated in the 1960s through a compelling piece of research that identified what was called the "Pygmalion effect."

In this research, conducted by Robert Rosenthal and Lenore Jacobson, three groups of randomly chosen children were assigned to three teachers. The teachers were told that the three groups of children were quite different. Group One was described as gifted and talented, a special group of children any teacher would be delighted to have in a classroom. Group Two was labeled as average, so teachers were told to expect average grades and few behavioral problems. Group Three was described as children with a history of behavioral problems who made poor grades—in other words, "Good luck dealing with these misfits."

You can probably already see where this is heading. All the randomly assigned groups of kids behaved in just the manner that the teachers "saw" them. The researchers created a self-fulfilling prophecy. The view the teachers held of the children was so powerful that the kids began to perform to match it, even though the view was not accurate. Rosenthal and Jacobson's book, *Pygmalion in the Classroom: Teacher Expectation and Pupils' Intellectual Development*, was first published in 1968 and was updated in 1992.

The importance of mirroring and the Pygmalion effect are important for us all to consider as parents and are particularly relevant to the formation of entitlement. Many wealthy people don't receive accurate or helpful feedback from their environment because they surround themselves with people who keep them insulated and tell them what they want to hear. They don't experience or even necessarily learn about the naturally occurring consequences of their behavior. Both children and adults may be treated with a degree of "specialness" that doesn't serve them well as a family or as individuals. Like third graders whose artwork is still being received with the oohs and aahs more appropriate to a three-year-old, they aren't given accurate information. As odd as it may sound, being treated as if you're so special that everything you do is just fine is not doing a child—or an adult—any favors.

In one of my interviews I met a delightful couple in their 60s who had raised two sons and a daughter. The daughter, Sofia, was obviously the apple of her dad's eye. He described her as "Daddy's little girl," and it was clear that he had a deep love for her. Both parents, in fact, clearly regarded her as uniquely special. The boys were allowed rough and tumble play and participated in sports. The parents assumed the sons could take care of themselves. They were required to work at summer jobs outside of the family business. Sofia, on the other hand, helped her dad in the business, where she was allowed to keep her own hours so she could "just get to be a kid." It was one of her brothers who was actually trained in the business and who eventually took over the firm.

Sofia's parents gave her a lot of attention, and as she grew up she also received a lot of attention from others for her looks and her wealth. At the time I talked to the parents, Sofia was nearly 40 and struggling. She was recently divorced, unemployed, depressed, and emotionally and financially dependent on her parents. In looking back, these parents realized they had actually harmed their daughter by making life too easy for her. They had prepared their sons for life but had protected their daughter from life. They had raised her to assume she was entitled to be treated as someone special.

This story is certainly not unique to affluent families. Yet financial wealth can act as another layer protecting children from the consequences of life. The family money can create an illusion that we are in fact special.

As painful as it is for us as parents, we need to let our children experience difficulties and struggle. It is the process that helps them learn to be resilient and confident. Ironically, not treating children with too much "specialness" is one of the ways to support them in discovering and developing the abilities and talents that make them genuinely special.

An Empowered Relationship with Money

What wealth creators want for their children is something I call "going from shirt sleeves to success." Research has consistently shown that 90% of all family wealth transfers fail by the end of the third generation. It's a world-wide phenomenon, across all cultures, and has been true for so many centuries that various countries have their own ways of describing it. In this country, the expression is "shirt sleeves to shirt sleeves in three generations." Other terms are "clogs to clogs" or "rice paddy to rice paddy" in three generations.

Stereotypically, the first generation is a self-made success who starts in a blue-collar business and builds wealth. By the time the grandkids are coming on the scene, much of the wealth has dissipated and the family is imploding or falling apart in some way. It's tragic, and it's what got me into this work. My focus is on helping families be successful together.

The challenge of raising kids in affluence without teaching them a destructive sense of entitlement has at its heart a paradox. The founding generations may have worked hard to achieve success and wealth. The qualities they held, which helped created the wealth, probably included hard work, delayed gratification, commitment to excellence, taking risks, and meeting challenges.

Yet money in and of itself was not necessarily their primary goal. The focus was on the process, product, or service that brought in the money. The members of the first and second generations may have developed the skills to create great wealth, but they didn't automatically develop the skills to manage that wealth or the insights to pass it along wisely to future generations.

Most of us, as parents and grandparents, want our children or grandchildren to have it easier than we did. We don't want them to have to struggle. Yet we also want them to learn and practice the values that helped make it possible for them to live easier lives. Ironically, it was through our own struggles that we learned many of those values. The challenge is to adapt those values to managing and living with wealth rather than creating it.

What we really want for future generations, of course, is "the best." The challenge is figuring out just what "the best" really is. It isn't necessarily a life of more money, more possessions, or more experiences. Nor is it a life of unrealistic and unnecessary deprivation. What it may be is the sense of balance that comes with an empowered relationship with money.

Money Relationship Continuum

Denial	Empowerment	Entitlement
Worry	Balance	Shame
Fear	Responsibility	Arrogance
Shame	Satisfaction	Carelessness
Ignorance	Intentionality	Dissatisfaction
Dissatisfaction	Gratitude	Dysfunction
Pretending money doesn't matter	Using money to support life purpose	Equating net worth and self worth

What does it mean to have an empowered relationship with money?

- It is living life as a responsible adult instead of allowing wealth to keep you a dependent child.
- It is knowing who you are and what matters to you, then using money to support your passions.
- It is enjoying wealth and appreciating the advantages it brings into your life. It's living with a sense of gratitude for those advantages: not having to struggle to pay the bills, being able to easily travel and enjoy other experiences, being free from worry about the financial future, having the ability to give easily and generously, being able to have luxurious things if you want them, knowing you can afford whatever medical care you might need, and being able to pursue whatever career paths and

interests appeal to you.

- It is not being ashamed of having wealth, but not being proud of it for its own sake, either. It is a sense of balance based on understanding that having money doesn't make you either better or worse than those who don't have it. It is understanding that net worth is not the same as self-worth.
- It is accepting the responsibility of managing wealth with conscious attention instead of using it carelessly or destructively.

Thriving families have many ways to help their members build healthy, empowered relationships with wealth. After working with and observing many of these families, I've learned that all those strategies build on the following five key factors:

1. Intentionality. Successful families say yes to wealth. They neither use it with destructive carelessness nor pretend it doesn't exist. They choose to accept both the advantages and the responsibility of wealth and to create a plan for the family money.
2. A focus on future generations. Successful families make a deliberate choice to train family members in stewardship and responsibility.
3. Open communication. Families who are able to talk about problems are the ones most likely to be able to solve those problems, and family members who communicate well build closer relationships. It is especially important for wealth creators to be open about their legacy intentions.
4. Creating a family brand/identity. A clear sense of "what this family stands for," articulated in a mission or purpose statement, provides a foundation for decision-making and invites family members to ally themselves with a positive, shared purpose under the family name.

5. Redefining success for subsequent generations. It is essential to transform the values and skills that created the wealth into the values and skills required to manage and live with it in healthy ways.

It is certainly true that wealth can foster a sense of entitlement, dissatisfaction, and dysfunction. It is equally true that wealth can foster responsibility, stewardship, and satisfaction. Many wealthy families flourish, achieve, and give back to their communities in significant ways. In later chapters we'll take a closer look at some of the strategies they use.

CHAPTER TWO
CREATING A HEALTHY FAMILY CULTURE

FIRST, THE BAD news. There is no magic formula guaranteed to leave your descendants a legacy of stewardship and financial health. There isn't a recipe or a set of rules to follow that will ensure your kids and grandkids end up making responsible, wise choices that support them in leading happy and productive lives.

Now for the good news. There is no magic formula guaranteed to leave your descendants a legacy of stewardship and financial health. There isn't a recipe or a set of rules to follow that will ensure your kids and grandkids end up making responsible, wise choices that support them in leading happy and productive lives.

Here's why the lack of a clear formula for success is both good and bad. Yes, there are guidelines and behaviors that can help families create and maintain healthier cultures. In my work with families, as well as in talking with members of wealthy families for this book, I have discovered some practices that are common to families that flourish. These practices are tools and habits that can be learned. This book is intended to help you learn them.

Valuable as these tools can be, however, they are not part of a rigid formula that will lead to success if you use all of them in precisely the right way and will lead to failure if you don't. Ultimately, creating a healthy family culture depends less on exactly what you do and more on how you do it and who you are. Building a legacy of wisdom and stewardship has more to do with the kind of person you are and the example you set than on following a set of rules about inheritances, charitable giving, and family governance.

From time to time I encounter a family that appears to be doing everything right. They have a system in place to manage the family wealth, they give to charities, they have family meetings, and they appear to be educating younger generations in stewardship. From the outside, they look really good. Yet on the inside, things don't feel right. Much of what they do comes out of rigidity, a need for control, and frozen expectations. It's no wonder, then, that members of the third or fourth generations may get angry, rebel, and behave badly.

Families also consult me, not because they are failing, but because they want to do better. They aren't necessarily struggling with serious dysfunction or destructive behaviors, but they know they could improve their communication and become more conscious in their stewardship of the family wealth. They want to help family members live happier, more fulfilled, and more rewarding lives. They aren't content to be "doing okay;" they want to flourish.

The most fundamental component of success and health as a family is the underlying attitude and belief system of its members. One quality emerges as a common theme for every flourishing family—integrity.

I found it fascinating that few of the family members I interviewed actually used the word "integrity." Yet most of them told me things like this:

- The real satisfaction of having a successful business isn't the money, it's a job well done.
- We set up a family foundation because we want to make a difference in the world.

- My father taught me there's honor in any job; the janitors' work is important to the company, too, and it's important to treat everyone with respect.
- Be humble—it's not about "me, me, me." This success and wealth was given to us by a higher power, and it's our responsibility to use it well.
- We have been so blessed; we want to give something back.

Families who base their wealth management on a foundation of integrity and a sense of having been blessed are the ones most likely to flourish. Most of these families practice most of the habits of healthy family cultures described in this chapter. The habits, however, are of limited value unless they grow out of the family's values. Yes, what you do as individuals and as a family matters. What matters even more is how you do it. The biggest secret to creating a family legacy of success is acting with a "big heart" and passing along your own integrity, passion, and values.

Assuming integrity as a base, then, here are ten patterns of belief and behavior that I've observed in families who successfully create healthy cultures.

Ten Habits of Healthy Family Cultures

1. Establish shared family values.

Values are the beliefs that represent a family to the outside world and, more importantly, to themselves. They are what the family stands for. One of the best descriptions of shared family values was one I heard from a man who was a fan of classic movies about the Old West. He called it "riding for the brand." Everyone in the family could relate to this phrase and understand its meaning—that it was an honor to be part of the family and, with that honor, the members bore the responsibility of living their values. The "brand" symbolized what the family stood for.

The key, of course, is not simply "riding for the brand," but building a brand that is worth riding for. There's nothing to be proud of if the outfit you work for is owned by a bully like the big open-range rancher who is the villain in so many old westerns. You don't want to ride for a brand that represents threatening to burn out homesteaders, illegally fencing off water holes, and rustling the neighbor's cattle. Instead, you want to ride for a brand that believes in keeping your word, helping those who need it, and doing the right thing even if it's the harder thing. You want your brand to uphold the "code of the West" in the highest sense.

Nor does "riding for the brand" mean all the members of the family need to spend their lives in the saddle on the home range. In flourishing families, it's just fine if some members go back East to school and become doctors or bankers. Or, for that matter, if they fence off their own quarter sections and become sodbusters. What matters is that they take the family values, honor, and integrity into whatever they choose to do.

In many cases, the personal values of the first-generation wealth creators include hard work, a commitment to excellence, willingness to sacrifice and take risks, and frugality. It's natural for those qualities to evolve into values that represent the family as a whole, but it isn't always easy to transfer them to later generations who grow up in affluence. In successful families, founding generations do more than expect younger members to live up to the family values. They find ways to consciously teach those values as well as modeling them in their own behavior. Families who flourish also understand that there are many ways to demonstrate values such as stewardship, hard work, and excellence. Such families are secure and flexible enough to accommodate varying lifestyles and behaviors because they focus on the values that underlie those surface appearances.

2. Define a family mission and vision.

Values are what a family believes to be important, and defining a family mission and vision is the first step in acting on those beliefs. When I work with families, we begin with a family values retreat. Our first task is to guide family members to unearth and document their strengths and core values. Based on those values, we then draft a family mission and vision statement. Putting the family mission into words helps people focus more clearly on living from their values. Family and individual goals, projects, and day-to-day actions become extensions of the family's core values.

There is no one "right" or "best" value to include in a family mission statement. It's common for these statements to include commitments like the following: to support family members in their individual growth, to use the wealth for the good of their community, to support specific causes such as education or medical research, to increase the family wealth, and to foster family closeness. A mission statement is intended to be an accurate reflection of what truly is important to a particular family. It will be of limited value if it is based on what family members think "should" be important according to their peers, society, or even the original creator of the wealth.

The mission statement acts as a touchstone for the family, providing a foundation for future decisions. Having a family mission is powerful because it compels a family to act in the best interest of the family and its desired future, rather than focusing on any one individual.

3. Establish healthy limits and boundaries.

A phrase I hear often from members of financially successful families, especially those in the first and second generations, is a desire to "Not act like rich people." They appreciate and enjoy the many benefits that wealth can bestow, but they don't want to be perceived as arrogant, selfish, or spoiled. They don't want to be set apart and labeled as "the rich." They don't want their children and grandchildren to grow up with a sense of entitlement instead of a sense of responsibility. They understand that having no restrictions on what they can do and have is not a healthy environment for either children or adults.

Flourishing families don't pretend their wealth doesn't exist or refuse to use it, but they choose to live relatively ordinary lives. Adults practice the value of restraint by setting reasonable limits and boundaries for themselves in both financial and nonfinancial ways. They set similar boundaries for their children in order to actively teach them responsibility and restraint.

Fundamentally there are two kinds of boundaries, internal and external. Internal boundaries are represented by developing our sense of self-esteem and our ability to set internal limits, e.g., setting limits on expressing our frustrations rather than thinking everyone needs to hear about them. External limits are represented by taking care of ourselves in the world and not letting people take advantage of us. Healthy family systems encourage individuals to develop a sense of self that is separate from the family. They support family members in finding their own voices.

4. Support family members in leading lives with purpose.

One of the greatest fears for many wealth creators is that their success will enable future generations to become dependent and live off the family money without becoming contributing members of society. The family mission statement is a crucial tool to create an environment that encourages responsibility and productivity instead of dependency. It is important for the family mission and vision statements to support family members' individual values and missions rather than stifling or imposing them. Many families define as one of the family values an expectation that family members will do something useful or productive even if they don't need to earn an income. Others actively involve younger generations in managing the family wealth or working with family foundations. Still others encourage family members to pursue the careers, interests, and goals they are passionate about, either within or outside of the family business interests.

"The privilege of a lifetime is being who you are."

Joseph Campbell

A primary drive of a human being is the drive to lead a purposeful life. Successful legacy families are very intentional in supporting each member of the family to live a life with purpose and meaning. The family isn't threatened by differences in personality, thought, or temperament. Instead, it values the differences and sees them as contributing to the strength of the family.

5. Prepare heirs to manage wealth in ways to foster well-being.

If you bought your son a Corvette for his 16th birthday but didn't teach him how to drive before you let him take it out on the road, whose fault would it be if he wrecked it? Turning large sums of money over to heirs without teaching them how to manage wealth is just as destructive as turning an untrained driver loose with a powerful sports car.

Families that flourish do active financial parenting with both young and adult children. When children are small, parents teach them the basics of money skills: setting aside money for saving, spending, and sharing. As the children approach their teen years, the parents begin teaching them how to earn money and keep a budget.

Teaching these basic money skills is difficult for all parents, but particularly for affluent families because the limits can seem so arbitrary. One client told me that growing up in an affluent family he felt there were no limits on spending because he knew his family could afford anything. His parents told him that he had to earn half of the money for his first car. He was incensed, because many of his friends were getting expensive cars for their 16th birthdays. His parents couldn't hide behind the rationale of "That's all we can afford." Instead, they used the experience as an opportunity to talk about the family value of earning your own way.

Parents in thriving legacy families teach children about managing money by setting appropriate limits on allowances and gifts, letting them learn from the consequences of their financial mistakes, and talking openly about the benefits and responsibilities of wealth. They allow and encourage adult children to grow up, and they seek out advisors to teach them about wealth management. Most importantly, members of older generations model responsible stewardship by educating themselves financially and being actively involved in managing the family money.

6. Practice skillful communication.

Good communication is probably the most essential habit for any family that wants to flourish. It's important to remember that the goal is effective communication, not perfect communication. Different families will have varying styles and methods of communication, different degrees of closeness, and different needs. What families who communicate well have in common is an intention to be clear and open. They avoid the manipulation, secrets, and power games that foster dysfunction and distrust. Instead, they have a commitment to transparency. They are willing to learn from each other, listen to one another, and create an atmosphere of tolerance for differences. They are willing to work together to resolve conflicts, with help from professionals as necessary.

Most families need help in this area. It certainly isn't enough to just say you need to improve your communication. In working with families, I teach specific communication skills as well as skills in conflict resolution and the neuroscience of communication. This gives families a new set of tools to use in communicating.

7. See the family as a learning system.

Families thrive when they have a foundation of defined family values, but it's important to see that foundation as a "floating floor" rather than a fixed slab of concrete. It needs to be a strong base that is also flexible enough to accommodate and encourage growth and change. Families who are most successful at passing their values on to future generations understand the importance of seeing mistakes as something to learn from. They are willing to learn from advisors and confident enough to seek out those who are willing to "speak truth to power." They cultivate a sense of appropriate humility.

The family also gets out of the way of natural consequences. As an example, suppose a college son or daughter blows through a whole semester's budgeted spending money in one month. For many parents, the first response is a temptation to send more money right away. Instead, the most helpful response is,

"Bummer. Sounds like you need to find a job."

Families who value learning also foster leadership among younger generations. They appreciate that members of both older and younger generations can learn from and teach each other.

8. See the family as a steward of the wealth.

The word "stewardship" is commonly associated with giving, but giving is actually only one facet of it. Stewardship, as defined by Merriam-Webster, is "careful and responsible management of something entrusted to one's care."

An individual who makes a fortune is likely to think originally in terms of "my money." This person has created the wealth and can dispose of it in any way he or she wishes. For later generations, however, eventually the wealth essentially takes on an identity of its own. It no longer belongs to the wealth creators or other individuals, but is "family money" in a larger sense. The responsibility of those who manage it is to be wise stewards, both preserving wealth for future generations and using it for a greater good.

Most of the legacy families that I have worked with or interviewed discuss openly the family's responsibility to be the steward of the wealth. There is a deep sense that "to whom much is given, much is expected." They describe themselves as the custodians of their wealth and of the well-being of others. I have worked with a number of families who had very different political or social beliefs from each other, but they were in alignment around the value of making a contribution in the lives of others.

9. Value giving back.

In my work with families, I have noticed a particular pattern that occurs again and again. I'll be talking with family members, usually members of the first or second generations, who are successful, hard-working creators or builders of the family wealth. They are capable, ambitious, no-nonsense business people who operate effectively in competitive environments.

Then they start talking about a charity they support or a family foundation. All at once they're using phrases like, "how blessed I am in my life," and "making the world a better place," and "how good it feels to give something back."

A sense of gratitude and a desire to give back are common in flourishing legacy families. Many of them set up charitable foundations to manage their giving. Others work through their churches, community organizations, or existing charitable organizations. In addition, many family members give generously of their time and expertise as well as their money.

10. Have a long-term view of the family.

Families that are successful in passing along their values as well as their wealth have a long-term view of the family. When families and their advisors begin talking about taking this long-term view, one common approach is to try and develop a 100-year plan. To begin with, I strongly suggest talking about 30 or at the most 50 years instead. I have found that families have a hard time getting their minds wrapped around the concept of "What we want to look like in 100 years." But most of us can think in terms of 30 years.

In many of the families I work with, the moms and dads aren't going to be around three decades from now. But they can look at their kids and grandkids and say, "Sure, I have an idea what I want this family to look like in 30 years." There is a strong awareness that they are investing in something now that is meant to serve the family for generations to come. Many of them compare this to planting a tree today that is only a sapling, but knowing that in generations to come it will provide shade and protection.

It's important for all adult members of the family to talk about the future, and this kind of thinking dramatically resets those conversations. They emphasize questions like these: What's your dream? What do you want to be looking back on 35 years from now? In the afterlife, whatever your concept of that may be, what do you want to be looking down and seeing in this family? This can open the door to some beautiful conversations that get to whatever is at the heart of things for the family. Instead of arguing over who gets what today, the focus becomes how the decisions that family members are making today will affect their grandchildren.

The focus shifts away from seeing the family money as an ATM for the purpose of allowing family members to withdraw whatever they want whenever they want it. Instead, the money becomes a shared asset and long-term resource to be tended and used responsibly. This frames the family legacy not just in terms of Generation One giving to Generation Two, which gives to Generation Three, and so on, but in a longer sense. Younger family members see themselves as givers as well as receivers.

While successful families stress a sense of family unity and shared values, it is equally important to encourage members of each generation to find their own way. Being a legacy family does not mean that everyone works in the family business or follows in the parents' footsteps. Instead, there is support for each person to be autonomous as well as identifying with the family. That diversity of thought and opinion strengthens the base of the family rather than being a threat. Individual family members get to choose whether they want to be in the business or contribute to the family legacy in other meaningful ways—not all of them financial. The high school teacher, stay-at-home parent, or artist in the family needs to be as esteemed as the investment banker or the son or daughter who is involved in the family business.

One important element of long-term thinking is open communication about inheritances. Allowing family members to live with "great expectations" can destroy their ambition, sap their energy, and create a destructive belief that whatever they do doesn't really matter. Letting children assume they will inherit much more than is actually the case is a sure way to leave a legacy of bitterness and resentment.

Many of the wealth creators I have worked with express strong beliefs that leaving vast sums to their children is not in the children's best interests. Instead, they consider it both an obligation and a privilege to be able to leave money for charitable purposes. Many of them talk about having been blessed with abundance and being grateful for the opportunity to help make the world a better place.

It is essential to be clear within the family about these legacy intentions. This goes beyond simply informing kids and grandkids that most of the money will be donated to the arts, the church, or the homeless. Instead, successful families involve children and grandchildren in legacy planning. One form this often takes is to establish foundations that give family members an opportunity to help make decisions about giving. At some point, usually into third and later generations beyond the creation of the wealth, the money evolves into "family money." Its ownership, and the responsibility for managing it and making decisions about it, belongs to the family as a whole rather than to one person or one generation.

The families that flourish develop a habit of supporting both individual development and the long-term health and sustainability of the family. They see the family as an entity in itself and think in terms of, "How do we provide care and sustenance to the family." This larger view orients the individual family members away from a self-serving view to a perspective of what is best for the long-term health of the family. It helps them realize they are part of something larger than themselves, something that is worthwhile and a source of pride.

Members of thriving families fundamentally see that their value is not in the definition of their financial wealth. Their value is in their relationships with each other and their community. One wealthy grandfather summed this up elegantly. He told me that his goal was not only to pay for his granddaughters' weddings, but to have the physical health to be able to dance with his granddaughters at their weddings.

CHAPTER THREE

FAMILY VALUES

"I define a successful family as one that knows who it is, what it stands for, and where it is going. Successful families manage themselves deliberately."

Charles Collier, in *Wealth in Families*

IF YOU COULD pick one thing, tangible or intangible, that is the most important to pass between generations, what would it be? A study on legacies commissioned by the Allianz Group in 2005 asked a similar question. The number-one choice was a sense of morality or ethics. It was followed closely by faith, religion, family rituals, last wills and instructions, and possessions from the parental home.

What's interesting about this research is the way it speaks to the basic psychology of families. At the end of our lives, what matters most is not how much money we made or who we were in the world. It's how our family regards us and that sense of legacy, ethics, faith, and tradition that they have received from us.

Flourishing families share a commitment to create a legacy of integrity and strong values. While the specific values vary from family to family, the ways different families build those values into lasting legacies have several common factors. Successful families develop a healthy family brand, redefine success for successive generations, teach later generations to honor the source of the family wealth, and develop effective ways to tell the family story and communicate their values.

Whatever the core values may be, a key to helping the family flourish is *intentionality*. Passing along the beliefs that define the family is not left to chance or considered to be something that "just happens." Family members have identified their core values, can articulate them clearly, and deliberately choose to teach those values to younger generations. This chapter describes some of the components of healthy family values, as well as some strategies for defining those values.

Develop a Healthy Family Brand

Imagine being part of an ordinary middle-class family whose last name happens to be Rockefeller. You know you aren't related to the wealthy family, because a great-uncle did a lot of genealogy research looking hard for a connection and didn't find one. Yet the Rockefeller name is so associated with money that you can't get away from it. You are so sick of the smart remarks and the not-quite-joking cracks about how you ought to pick up the tab that you've thought seriously about changing your name to Smith.

For most Americans, "Rockefeller" means "money." That's what is perceived as the family identity. The name itself is used as shorthand for wealth in the same way the name Scrooge is used to mean miserly or Einstein is used to symbolize genius. Yet if you asked several random people what they know about the Rockefeller family's businesses, charitable giving, or other activities, the answer would most likely be "nothing." The public image associated with the name may not have much to do with what members of the Rockefeller family really believe or do.

Wealthy families have little control over how others perceive them, and developing a healthy family brand isn't about the public image. It isn't about trying to create a positive public relations "spin" or cover up flaws. The brand is for family members, not outsiders. It's essential for wealthy families to consciously define their identity as a first step toward passing on core family values.

"What we stand for" may vary a great deal from family to family. Some may place great importance on involving members of later generations in a family business, while others strongly discourage it. Some may focus on charitable giving through family foundations or trusts, while others emphasize building and preserving the family wealth. Some emphasize family closeness, and others don't. Each family has a set of beliefs that identify the family both to themselves and to the larger world.

Interestingly, in all the families I've worked with, I've never had anyone describe having money for its own sake as a core value. Financial security may be a value, and so may a commitment to preserve and increase the family wealth. A number of families that I work with want to support their children in having empowered relationships with wealth where it affords them opportunities but doesn't disable or undermine their ability to forge their own identity. Some families may want the wealth to follow the bloodline, while others value the diversity of including in-laws. Whatever the financial values may be, it is important for families to be clear about them, just as they are about other core values.

The values that seem most important in most families focus on family relationships, individual satisfaction and happiness, spirituality, stewardship, and giving back.

Defining Success

"The wealth of a family consists in the human and intellectual capital of its individual members. A family's financial capital

is a tool to support the growth of the family's human and intellectual capital."

James E. Hughes, *Family Wealth — Keeping It in the Family*

Jay Hughes is regarded as the pioneer of family wealth consulting. *Family Wealth — Keeping It in the Family* is seen as the seminal book in this area. In it he suggested an idea that at the time was innovative but that we now tend to take for granted. Affluent families have historically seen themselves through just one lens, their financial capital. Jay said that we really need to look at families and have them look at themselves within a broader theoretical context. We need to see families as having human, intellectual, and social capital. In conversations, Jay and others have added physical and spiritual capital as well.

This mindset is the basis of self-awareness in families. It broadens the base to help them see themselves beyond just their financial capital. It encourages family members to talk about what's really important to them and to see each other as having strengths in areas other than financial.

Financial net worth is only one small part of the total worth of any family. In a broader sense, the "human and intellectual capital" of a family includes many things: the intelligence, talents, skills and knowledge of each family member; the social networks and influence of family members and the family as a whole; and the family's reputation. Flourishing families value all of these types of capital and include them in the balance sheet of intangibles that measures what we might call Family Net Worth.

In order to honor and make full use of all the family capital, it's essential for a family to actively define not only its values, but also what it regards as "success." In many cases, the people that are valued the most in the family are the ones who are in the family business. This is a common source of conflict and pain. Families that thrive, on the other hand, tend to define success and value much more broadly. They respect and appreciate the contributions of those who are not part of the family business, but who have gone their own way. They understand that what is done by the craftsman, the schoolteacher, or the stay-at-home mom is as valuable as what is done by the CEO or top salesman in the family business. One family, for example, regarded the first-generation mother and grandmother as its "chief emotional officer."

It's crucial to acknowledge the distinction between the family's *values* and the *behaviors* through which different members of the family carry out those values. For members of the wealth-building generations, values such as hard work and commitment lead to successes that are easy to measure by a financial yardstick. Later generations may hold the same values but apply them in different ways. The key is to pay more attention to the underlying values behind someone's behavior than to the surface behavior. A later-generation young adult may not be working hard at a job or may not be "successful" in the same way that the wealth creators defined success, yet still may be living according to the family's deeper values.

"Hard work" as a value for the generation that built the wealth might translate to a value of "productivity" for later generations. This could include actively helping manage the family money or a charitable foundation, working in the family business or having a separate career, or not necessarily holding a job at all. Besides paid employment, other ways to be productive might include being active in community organizations, pursuing fulfilling hobbies and activities, or focusing on raising one's own children. It isn't necessary to have a career to be productive in worthwhile ways.

Some families have "entrepreneurship" as a value, and they act on it by using family resources to support individuals in building their own businesses and careers. One method is to have a family bank for the purpose of supporting entrepreneurial passion. In this concept, a family member who has a business idea goes to the family bank with the idea. There will be a committee of family members and outsiders, including someone who has expertise in the area under consideration. The individual writes up a business plan and makes a formal request. The committee will only invest in the idea if it has merit and would be a worthy investment of the family's money.

A value of "taking worthwhile risks" may have been an important component in creating the original wealth. For members of later generations, risk-taking might include stepping outside of the comfort zone of expectations around how a member of a wealthy family "should" behave. This could include following their passions for music, arts, travel, or exploration. It might mean joining the Peace Corps or helping build schools or clinics in poor areas by swinging a hammer themselves as well as giving money.

A value of "humility" could be carried out by behavior such as living within one's means, being respectful of other people regardless of their relative wealth or position, and choosing not to use wealth to bully or manipulate others.

One of the strongest values in many flourishing families is a sense of gratitude. Wealth creators commonly talk about being "blessed" by the financial rewards for their efforts, rather than regarding their financial success with arrogance or pride. Later generations emphasize living with the awareness that being born into wealth is in many ways a matter of luck rather than merit. These families embody the principle that "to whom much is given, much is expected." This sense of gratitude and of having been blessed drives them to give back to their communities through charitable giving and in many other ways.

Gratitude is a powerful offset to entitlement, yet it is a concept that doesn't come naturally for most of us. We have a natural tendency to focus on what is wrong or what annoys us rather than appreciating what we liked about our day or what we appreciate about each other. Gratitude is like a muscle that needs exercise.

We can build gratitude in ourselves and our families by developing the practice of ending our day with what we are grateful for or asking the family to share an appreciation for each member of the family. A good resource is the book *Thanks!: How the New Science of Gratitude Can Make You Happier*, by Robert Emmons.

It's important for wealth creators to be open to broadening the family definition of "success" to encompass much more than just career achievement or financial productivity. Here are a few examples of different ways that members of wealthy families might be considered successful.

Alec is a fourth-generation member of a wealthy family that values ambition, success, and giving back. His brother and several cousins are employed in the family business, but Alec has chosen to teach elementary school instead. He loves his work and excels at it. His wife, Madison, is thriving as a stay-at-home mom to their four young children. Alec's income from the family business and a trust fund established by his grandparents gives this couple the gift of financial independence. Alec is able to pursue the career he wants despite its relatively low pay. Madison is able to focus on the children. They don't live lavishly, but they certainly enjoy a much more comfortable standard of living than they would without the family money. They don't have to scramble to pay the bills or choose a living wage over job satisfaction. In addition, they use some of their wealth to support a charity that is important to them and in which they are personally involved. As parents, Alec and Madison are actively teaching their children the values of giving and being responsible.

Jessica is a talented musician whose primary instrument is the hammer dulcimer. She is part of a small folk group that plays at fairs, music festivals, and other small venues. Performing by itself isn't enough to provide members of the group with even a minimal living, so most of them have other "real" jobs. Jessica's income from her trust fund allows her to focus on the music she loves and protects her from the struggles that are common to musicians, especially those who are out of the mainstream. She has also chosen to produce several albums of the group's music, even though she has yet to sell enough copies to cover her costs.

As teenagers, Steven and his sister Kathryn both had part-time jobs in the family business. Steven began working there full-time as soon as he got his college degree, and eventually he succeeded his father as CEO. Kathryn, on the other hand, focused after college on raising her own children. She always felt a little left out of the family and less successful than her brother. Then, in her mid-30s, she started getting involved in the family foundation. Her involvement ignited a passion for philanthropy. She went on to become the board's most active member and eventually became the head of the family council. Kathryn never made a lot of money, but her contribution to the community and the long-term success of the family was significant. It was rewarding to see the pride she developed as both she and her brother recognized that, together, they were protecting the legacy of the family.

Two common threads run through these stories. First, all these members of wealthy families are doing something positive, even though they may not be reaping any financial rewards. They are actively using their abilities in ways that matter to them. This is not the same as being a dilettante who dabbles in art, writing, or business without any particular motivation, commitment, or satisfaction.

Second, they are taking advantage of the financial independence that the family money gives them. The money frees them from the necessity to earn a living and allows them to spend their time doing what they love.

Wealth creators who spent long hours, weeks, and years building up successful businesses may have trouble accepting this freedom as "success." Where is the hard work? Where is the financial reward? Where is the career recognition?

What no one in the family may consider is the possibility

that these members of later generations could be doing just what the original creators of the wealth did. In many cases, they do work hard. They are following their passions and doing exactly what they want to do. Much of the time, that's precisely what the wealth creators did. What I see and hear over and over from wealth creators is that success to them wasn't about the money. What drove them were the challenges of building businesses, the pleasure of using their talents, the satisfaction of providing a service, or the enjoyment of "playing the game" and winning. The money—just as it is with members of later generations—was a secondary reward.

Honoring the Source

A common concern in wealthy families is the increasing separation between younger generations and the original source of the family money. Great-Grandfather may have gotten his coveralls dirty in the oil fields or spent long hours behind a desk managing complex business details. He and Great-Grandmother may have mortgaged everything they owned in support of their dreams or personally served customers they knew by name. The original family values such as frugality, hard work, and responsibility most often grew out of necessity as the founders invested their most valuable resources—their time, energy, and talent—in their work.

For members of third, fourth, or later generations, the founding of the family fortune may seem as remote as the history of the American Revolution. Stories about the risks Great-Granddad took to get his small-town furniture store started may seem as distant as stories about cowboys driving cattle across the Great Plains—and a lot less exciting. To someone growing up in a lifestyle that includes household staff, more than one home, overseas vacations, and a family jet, the mundane details of where the money comes from may seem uninteresting or irrelevant.

A common value in thriving wealthy families is teaching a sense of respect and appreciation for the source of the wealth. Fostering that respect and appreciation takes many forms, but here are some important factors to consider:

1. Teaching members of later generation to value a family business is not the same as expecting them to participate in it. Some flourishing families encourage younger members to find careers within the family business, while others actively discourage it. Neither approach is right or wrong. What matters most is that the choices are made in ways that support good health for both the business and the family.

2. Succession planning and estate planning need to be done in ways that acknowledge the different needs, contributions, and participation of family members who work in the business and those who don't.

3. If families own businesses, it is crucial to keep family members aware that the business depends on the efforts of all the employees. In thriving families, the mindset is that members of the family support the employees of the business, rather than vice versa. This is often communicated with statements like these: "My grandfather always told us there is honor in any job. He used the company's janitor as an example of someone whose work made an important difference for the company." "My parents talked about how important it was to treat employees with respect and pay them well." "One of my father's strengths as a leader was his courtesy and the way he listened to the people who worked for him." "My dad said he may have owned the business, but he thought of his clients as his bosses."

4. Many flourishing families familiarize children with the

family business from the time they are young by taking them to visit and introducing them to employees. It often works best to teach children how the business functions, not by lectures or direct explanations, but by allowing them to see parents' involvement in the business as a normal part of everyday life. One client told me about a time he had a chance to observe his father negotiate a business deal. The son was in college, which he realized in retrospect had been a critical time in his life. He was trying to make sense of who he was as a man and learn how to say no, set limits, and be his own person while being respectful of others. He told me how important it was to see his father negotiate from a place of authority and self-respect while respecting the other person's point of view. He saw how his father could be strong, yet flexible and appreciative of different perspectives. What he learned from this was especially powerful because he saw and heard his father model this behavior. The lesson wasn't just words, but action that he was able to observe and later emulate in his life.

5. Money can seem like such an abstraction, particularly the further the family is removed from the wealth creator. That's why the factors above also apply if the primary "family business" is managing the family money. Part of financial parenting is teaching children about investing and money management, helping them understand that stewardship of the family wealth is also an active business.

It's crucial to provide experiences for later generations of sitting on the investment committee or spending time at the family office really understanding the inner and financial machinery of the family and its wealth management. Most of us don't understand how money works, what a diversified portfolio is, or the difference between a stock and bond and why are both important. Just because someone has grown up around financial wealth doesn't mean they understand money. Exposing and educating the generations about money is a crucial survival skill that needs to be consciously taught.

In some families, the wealth may be based on an original inheritance that was the result of one person's exceptional talent and success. In others, it may come from a business that is still owned and operated by family members. Either way, it is essential for later generations to understand that the money isn't just "there." Real people did real work to earn it originally. Others have added to and taken care of it in subsequent generations. People still work for it, take risks for it, invest it, manage it, and continue to earn it in many other ways.

In some families, not all the values that helped create the original wealth are comfortable for members of later generations. One scenario I see from time to time is contemporary generations holding different political, social, and environmental views from those of the wealth creators. For example, I've worked with several families where the original wealth came from oil or mining, and some of today's family members hold the opinion that this was "raping the land."

This creates a serious inner conflict: "How can I enjoy the fruits of Great-Grandfather's labor when I believe what he did to get it wasn't right?" This ambivalent relationship with the wealth, subconsciously seeing it as more of a liability than an asset, is likely to lead to their squandering it. Part of my work with family members in this position is to get them to see the wealth creator less one-dimensionally and within the context of his own times. Perhaps the way he operated his business would not be acceptable to his descendants today, but he lived in a different world. Maybe he also cared deeply about his children and grandchildren and made many sacrifices for the family. He may also have used his wealth to give back to his community in many important ways.

I also ask them to consider that it may be easier to blame Great-Grandfather for the ways he created the wealth than to focus on developing their own empowered personal relationship with the wealth. Their responsibility to the family and the wealth is different from his, and it requires them to step up in their own lives. I encourage them to consider the ways they can be good stewards of it here and now.

Telling the Family Story

It was an illicit high-school drag race right out of *American Graffiti*. Gary, one of the spectators, was excited about a flashy hot rod that looked like a winner. His friend Todd, who knew the owners of the vehicles, told him, "No way." The other, far more ordinary-looking car would win. Its owner hadn't put his time and money into a sexy exterior to show off. Instead, he focused on what mattered—the power under the hood. For Gary, this incident became an analogy for the values that defined his life. Being the quietly competent "sleeper" instead of the "showoff" helped him become a successful and wealthy business owner. The story of the drag race, told and retold among his children and later his grandchildren, was one way of passing along that value.

Frank had started a bank in a small prairie town during the 1920s. He was well on his way to success until his bank failed during the Great Depression of the 1930s. He made a commitment to personally pay back every depositor who had lost money in the bank failure. Over the succeeding years, as he rebuilt the bank into a thriving enterprise, he repaid everyone he could locate. When he died in the 1960s, his will included a bequest to the town library equal to the amount owed to depositors he had been unable to find. This legacy of integrity was passed down to his children and grandchildren as an integral part of the family lore.

Each family has its own stories, and in wealthy families stories about how the original wealth creators became successful are part of the foundation of the family. Great-Grandma ignoring the experts and choosing the site to drill the oil well that started the family fortune. Grandma and Grandpa living in a curtained-off area at the back of their first drugstore. Great-Uncle working in a laundry to pay for his college education.

Telling these stories can be powerful ways to pass along the family's values and keep later generations in touch with the family's roots. They can be used intentionally and purposefully as teaching tools to help define and maintain the family identity.

Family rituals and traditions are another means of passing along values. One family developed summer vacations around a theme, with a scavenger hunt or "treasure map" game for the children that encouraged them to work hard to gain a reward. Each challenge was usually related to acts of kindness or giving, so the kids' most important reward was the satisfaction of doing something for others.

Other families make a point of involving even young children in their charitable giving. Some do this by example, allowing the kids to see what they give and being open about their giving rather than keeping it secret. Others involve children more actively, especially as they get older. One family made a "secret angel" ritual a part of their Christmas celebration, involving the children and later the grandchildren in choosing a local charity or family that needed help. The family challenge was to find creative ways to give to them without getting caught.

I've seen families who teach children about investing by giving them birthday gifts of small amounts of stock each year. Then the birthday celebration in subsequent years includes an assessment of how their birthday investment portfolios are doing.

Touchstone phrases that become informal family mottos

are another way to pass along family values. For Gary, the drag race story at the beginning of this section resulted in a family phrase, "It's what's under the hood that counts." Another family reminded themselves not to blame or whine with, "It's your own damn fault." This was used with a sense of empowerment and humor, rather than shaming or scolding, as a way of encouraging family members to focus on solving problems rather than avoiding them. Another family used "Job well done" to emphasize the satisfaction of doing something well over an external reward such as financial compensation.

Another family I worked with sold the business that had been in the family for generations. Their biggest question was how to help future generations stay true to the family core values of hard work and taking pride in what you do when there was no longer a business to work in. They came up with the mantra, "Stay true to your roots." For years to come, this served as a way to frame the stories about the importance of holding to the values that had made the family successful for generations.

Family Values Retreat

In my work with families, one of the most essential tools is the family values retreat, designed to help families create a mission or vision statement. The following description of this process is based on the three-generational structure that is typical of most of my clients. Much of the time, the family members who come to me for coaching are the husband and wife who are the original wealth creators. They are usually in their 60s, at an age where they are looking toward their own retirement and are concerned about leaving a legacy of financial empowerment instead of entitlement for their children and grandchildren.

My first step is to meet with Mom and Dad for several hours to help them clarify their deepest values and articulate them in the form of a mission statement. One concern that couples often bring up at first is, "Oh, we've already done that." They may have a mission statement written down somewhere, but they may not regard it as very important or useful. Quite often they don't even remember what it says.

The process we go through is intended to dig much deeper. In every values retreat I've done with a couple, even those who have been married for many years, the spouses have learned things about each other that surprised them. Meeting with a third person encourages each partner to tell stories they may never have told each other before. The process I use relies on powerful, unexpected questions. I don't follow a script, because I want the conversation to be as organic as possible and make the interview a discovery process. I may ask questions like these: How did you first meet? What about the other person caused you to say, "This is the one"? What do you most appreciate about your partner? What are the essential values that you see in your partner? Who most influenced you in your life? Tell me about that person and his or her values. How do you hope you will be remembered?

This process allows spouses to pause and examine their stories, history, motives, and underlying purpose in new and different ways. Most couples find it relatively painless and even exciting. While we all say we know what our values are, we often haven't really articulated them. Our goal is to unearth and examine their deepest values, then to use those values to draft a clear mission statement about what they stand for and what they really hope to see in the family long-term.

The next step is a family meeting that includes Mom and Dad, all the children and their spouses, and all the grandchildren older than about 14 to 16. Mom and Dad introduce their mission statement to the rest of the family and invite them to be part of it and expand it. The goal here is to include everyone's voices in the mission statement and foster a sense that everyone has a place in the family. It is essential for each person, including the members of the youngest generation, to have a chance to contribute. In order for the family to be successful, the members need to understand and agree on the basic foundational principles that the family stands for.

This part of the process may sound time-consuming and exhausting. Yet what I have found is that, once Mom and Dad have clarified their values during the initial values retreat and written a clear initial mission statement, fine-tuning the statement to incorporate suggestions from the rest of the family can often be done in just an hour or two.

If this process is truly going to be useful, it is essential for the mission statement to reflect the values the family actually holds, rather than ones family members feel they "should" hold. A value of "fostering family unity," for example, may be very important to one family but less so to another. Charitable giving may be a top priority for some families and less important for others.

It's easy to put together a generic mission statement full of praiseworthy values that sound good. That kind of statement, however, is exactly the one that will be forgotten and ignored. This is why it is so crucial in the initial values retreat to uncover the deep, genuine core values that family members actually live by.

It's also essential to keep in mind that the family mission statement is a living document that is likely to need updating and revising over time. Early generations may live by specific religious precepts that no longer apply for members of later generations. Values such as support for education or environmental issues might evolve over the years as the focus of the family's charitable giving shifts. Evaluating the mission statement regularly at family meetings, and updating it as appropriate, can help the family adjust its focus and reconsider its priorities. At the same time, this reassessment can keep family members in tune with the family's essential core values.

Sample Family Mission/Vision Statements

The following family mission or vision statements are typical of those created by families I have worked with. While some of the examples are based on the mission statements of real families, they have all been adapted and combined in order to protect client families' confidential information.

Our mission is to encourage and empower family members to live fulfilling, productive lives through honoring our core values of discipline, moderation, achievement, and community involvement. We want to pass those values on to future generations so the wealth they inherit will foster their ability to succeed rather than stifling it.

This family's mission is to manage our wealth wisely in order to preserve and increase it for future generations.

Our family mission is to make our communities better places by using our individual abilities and by contributing money wisely through our charitable foundation.

The mission of our family is to support each person in living with a sense of gratitude and stewardship, recognizing that we have been greatly blessed and that we have an obligation to use our emotional, intellectual, and spiritual resources as well as our financial resources to make a difference in the lives of others.

Our mission is to live according to the family heritage of honesty and integrity, to pass that heritage on to future generations, to help individual family members develop their unique abilities, and to give back to society.

Our first priority is to foster family unity and build healthy relationships within the family. Then, together, we can use our wealth and other resources prudently to support our values of providing opportunities in education and the arts to those with limited resources of their own.

The purpose of our wealth is to help family members enjoy and enrich their lives by developing their individual talents as well as their social, spiritual, and financial resources. Our core values include giving back to society with a sense of joy and gratitude.

Our family purpose is to lead a fulfilling life full of integrity where we effectively empower others to actively live up to their potential

Conclusion

Ultimately, leaving a legacy of strong family values comes down to one fundamental idea: living life with integrity and a sense of responsibility. The most important way for each generation in a family to transmit that value is to live it as an integral part of their everyday lives.

CHAPTER FOUR

INTENTIONAL FINANCIAL PARENTING

"IT IS A good idea to talk with your children about money." Do you agree or disagree with that statement?

Most likely, you agree. According to a 2005 survey by the Allianz Group, 75% of affluent Americans believe that talking with children about money is a good idea. The same survey, however, reported the number of parents who have actually talked about money with their kids: 34%. Just because we think we ought to discuss money with our kids doesn't mean we know how to do it.

Talking about money is hard. Research shows it to be harder than talking about sex. No wonder money is the number-one topic that couples fight about. Since couples have such difficulty discussing money with each other or managing it together, it makes sense that money is also a huge challenge for us when it comes to parenting. Yet financial parenting is an essential part of preparing our children to be competent adults who are capable of living fulfilled and rewarding lives. This is especially true in wealthy families. Taking on the challenge of financial parenting means getting over our discomfort with talking about money.

This discomfort isn't the only reason so many of us struggle to do a good job of teaching our kids about money. Let's face it—financial parenting, like any parenting, is hard work. It takes time and effort, and at times it also forces us to look at our own attitudes and assumptions about the role of money in our lives. It's all too easy for us to postpone or neglect our kids' financial education, or to assume their schools will take care of it. Basic money knowledge is such a fundamental life skill that schools certainly ought to teach it—my own belief is that it should be required for high school graduation. Since that is not the case, it's up to us as parents to teach money skills to our children.

If we want our children to grow up to become responsible with their money, we need to teach them the basics: Spending, Saving, and Sharing. I also believe it's important, even for kids in affluent families, to include Earning. All kids need to learn some nuts-and-bolts information about interest, how banking works, and the fundamentals of investing and budgeting.

Even more important are some broader concepts that at first glance may not seem to be directly related to managing money. Yet they are essential components in learning to use money wisely as the important tool it is. They are: allowing kids to struggle, understanding different money personalities, setting limits and boundaries, communicating openly about money, and modeling the money behavior you want your kids to learn.

The Necessity of Struggle

In wealthy families, it's necessary for the parents to have a strong commitment to letting kids experience and learn from their own consequences. That commitment often requires time and effort on the part of the parents. They need to actively choose to take the path that will help the kids learn and grow, instead of the much easier path of simply writing a check.

An old story describes a boy who was playing outside and found a butterfly just beginning to emerge from its chrysalis. He watched for a long time, becoming more and more worried about the insect as it struggled to free itself. Finally, afraid the butterfly was hopelessly trapped, he tore open the chrysalis to set it free. The insect's body was swollen with fluid that was meant to flow into and expand its wings. Yet, as the butterfly sat and feebly fluttered its wings, they never expanded. The struggle to emerge from the chrysalis was what helped force the fluid from the body into the wings. Without that struggle, the butterfly would never be able to fly.

Similarly, when a baby bird is ready to hatch, it uses a sharp projection on the end of its beak called the "egg tooth" to peck its way out of the eggshell. This process can take as much as a day and is exhausting. Yet during this time, the chick's lungs are beginning to function and become acclimated to breathing outside air. If a shell is so hard that the chick can't peck its way out, the chick will die. On the other hand, if someone interrupts the process by breaking open the shell too soon, the chick will be thrust into the outside world before it is ready. It will have trouble breathing and may not survive.

Both these stories illustrate what can happen when children have too much done for them. As parents, we want to make life easier for our children. We don't want to see them struggle, suffer, or fail. Yet most of us also realize that, if we do too much to ease their way, they won't be equipped to function in the world. They will have trouble making the transition from helplessness to competence. They may never develop the confidence and strength to take the risks that are necessary for them to learn to fly.

A term developed by British pediatrician and psychoanalyst D. W. Winicott for the balance between helping kids too much and not helping them enough is "optimal frustration." As human beings, we thrive when we have a certain level of struggle. We need challenges that help us develop our abilities. We need to make mistakes and experience failure in order to realize we can overcome and learn from them. We need to learn how to solve problems. We need to develop the flexibility to accommodate ourselves to inconvenience, interruption, and the reality that other people have needs, too. We need to figure out that the world is not all about us.

At the same time, we can't thrive and learn if our lives are so filled with difficulties that we are beaten down and come to believe we can't succeed. We need the chance to learn from our failures, but we also need the chance to learn from our successes. It's good if our paths have a few stumbling blocks, but not so many that we find them insurmountable road blocks instead.

All of us need practice in doing things that are hard or not fun or that we don't want to do. This is a common pitfall for bright kids who easily get As in school without any effort. If they are never faced with challenges that require them to work hard, they can get used to getting by with "good enough." They may learn to avoid anything hard—in part because they're afraid they might fail and in part because it's human nature to take the easier path. The same dynamic applies for kids who never have to struggle financially. They don't learn how to make money choices, to do without, or to plan and save in order to get something they want.

The challenge for parents is to find the middle way between making kids' lives too easy and saddling them with frustration just for the sake of frustration. It's one of those parenting tasks that require us to make our best guess, time and time again, as to when we should step in and help and when we should allow kids to work through their own difficulties. There is no "rule" for knowing the right choice—which can generate a level of frustration for parents that doesn't feel "optimal" at all.

Tony's parents had to make such a choice when, halfway through the first semester of his third year of college, their son ran out of money. His parents had agreed to pay for his tuition, housing, and books, but he was required to provide his own spending money. The money from his summer construction job could have seen him through the school year had he been frugal, but by the end of October he had spent it all.

Because his parents had allowed him to experience struggles while he was growing up, Tony knew better than to ask them for the money. Their commitment to pay his college costs was generous enough, and he knew they would expect him to live up to his side of the bargain. He dealt with the consequences of his own overspending by taking out a school loan. Since he had to get some financial information from his parents in order to get the loan, he had to admit to them that he had been irresponsible with his finances. Ideally, the embarrassment of that admission, plus the need to pay back the loan, would help Tony learn to budget more carefully in the future.

In one sense, Tony's mistake had consequences for his parents as well as himself. They had to spend some time and effort helping him with the process of getting the loan. Since the family had enough money so the parents could have afforded to give Tony an allowance, it would have been easier just to write him a check for the rest of the year's living expenses. Instead, they made a deliberate choice to let him solve his own budgeting problem by taking out the loan.

Choosing not to make children's lives too easy is one way of demonstrating that we respect them enough to allow them to learn from their own struggles. We all need to develop our own identities and find our own ways, and being faced with challenges and overcoming them is an important part of the process. When we make our children's paths too smooth, we deprive them of the chance to make their own "hero's journey." One of the most loving things we can do for our children is to help them learn from the consequences of their choices by surrounding them with reasonable limits.

Money Personalities

Any parent with more than one child has experienced one of
the shocking revelations of parenthood. With the first child,
you make your mistakes, you struggle, and eventually—at least
part of the time—you figure out what works and what doesn't.
When the second child comes along, you have more confidence,
because by now you think you know a little bit about what
you're doing. That confidence lasts until you run into a situation
that you learned how to manage successfully with the first child.
Optimistically, you apply the same solution—and it doesn't
work. You soon learn that a distressing amount of your hard-
learned parental expertise simply won't apply, because the second child is a different person than the first.

One of the areas where kids are very different is money. Each
of us has a unique "money personality." The more I work with
different client families as well as my own children, the more I
believe that major parts of those money personalities are both
innate and learned. Many money beliefs and behaviors are
learned from messages we receive from our parents, other influ-
ential adults, and society in general. Some of our money behaviors, though, appear to grow out of our essential selves. In many
families, you'll find one or two kids who seem to be naturally
frugal. They will stash away their birthday money without being
told to, and they think opening their own savings account at a
real bank is the next best thing to getting a puppy. A sibling may
be just the opposite. If you go on a vacation and on the first day
you give each child $20 in spending money, within an hour this
kid will have spent every dime on a plastic sword and be jabbing
everyone with it.

These are just two of the most obvious differences in the way
various people relate to money. For more information about
money personalities and styles, a good resource is the book
Money Harmony by psychotherapist and author Olivia Mellan
(www.moneyharmony.com).

To effectively teach kids about money, it helps to use different strategies with different money personalities. This is complicated by the fact that parents have unique money personalities, just as children do. The average family offers plenty of opportunities for misunderstandings and conflicts. Invariably at least one of our children will have a money personality that is in direct conflict with our own. The following suggestions serve as a guide to keep the money conversations purpose-driven as opposed to emotionally charged.

1. Start by identifying your own money personality as well as some of the early messages and experiences that may have shaped your beliefs about money. Spending some time exploring your own money beliefs is an important step in building your own empowered relationship with money. You may find it worthwhile to spend some time with a financial coach or therapist to learn how to reframe money messages that don't serve you well. The more balanced and comfortable you become in the way you relate to money yourself, the more effective a financial parent you can be.

2. Identify what you see as your children's money personalities. Do they tend to save money, want to earn it, spend it impulsively, worry about it, or avoid it?

3. Pay attention to the money messages you are giving to your children, through what you say and especially through what you do. Once you know what these messages are, you can begin to be more intentional about what you teach in both your words and your example.

4. Recognize that different money personalities aren't necessarily good or bad. Someone with a frugal personality may be wise in saving for the future, but may also be unnecessarily self-denying or ungenerous and may have trouble spending money even in responsible ways. The spender may be happy-go-lucky to the point of

irresponsibility, but may also be generous, optimistic, and more able to live in the present.

5. Understand that different money personalities will require different strategies.

    Kids who are savers, for example, may benefit from help with setting goals for their saving instead of saving for its own sake. They may also need encouragement to spend some of their money on things they want. It's a good idea to make sure they aren't manipulating other people into spending money when they should be using their own. Getting them involved in giving of both their time and their money is also helpful.

    For spenders, parents may need to insist that they save a certain percentage of their money and even help them set up ways to put savings aside first before they even get their hands on money to spend. Encourage them to give in ways that are more deliberate than impulsive by, for example, helping them research specific charities. Perhaps the hardest but most important strategy with spenders is not to bail them out. Be firm about enforcing limits and allowing them to experience their own consequences.

6. Recognize situations where the differences between parents' and kids' money personalities can be volatile. If your money personality and that of a child clash so strongly that you can't effectively teach that child, it may help to involve someone else as a mentor for either or both of you.

7. In addition to money personalities, it's also helpful to be aware of individual learning styles. Children who are more left-brained will like concrete steps, rules of thumb, and a good plan. If kids are more right-brained they will learn better through metaphors, stories, and asking them to check in with their intuition. A step-by-step plan will drive them crazy.

The goal of financial parenting is to help kids find their own paths to healthy money behavior. Those paths won't all be the same, and they don't need to be. It's essential for parents to work together, with help from others as necessary, to develop strategies that support the kids' individual differences while you help them work toward balance and responsibility.

Setting Limits and Living within Your Means

For most families, lack of money sets its own limits. Sometimes parents don't even need to say no; it's perfectly obvious that the family budget simply doesn't have room for private voice lessons, a trip to Hawaii for spring break, or a new car for high school graduation. Middle-class kids with middle-class friends will probably just assume such luxuries are out of reach.

Kids from wealthy families know better. They understand that their parents have no need to say no for financial reasons. The challenge for parents, then, is to say no for other reasons and make it stick. Since there are few real financial limits, parents need to set limits in other ways.

The most essential way to do this is through example. One common characteristic of families who manage wealth successfully is living within their means. As one second-generation owner of a flourishing family business put it, "We don't go around acting like rich folks."

For families with more than enough wealth to do or have anything they could ever think of wanting, the very idea of "living within your means" may seem absurd. On a strictly dollars-and-cents level, it probably is. Emotionally, however, living within limits is an essential part of raising children to be healthy, functional adults.

Living within your means has different meanings to different families. One way to think of it is making a choice to live in the middle or lower level of your financial comfort zone rather than the high end. The term "financial comfort zone" comes from the book *Wired for Wealth* by Brad Klontz, Ted Klontz, and Rick Kahler. They describe it as the financial "neighborhood" you inhabit, within which you and the people around you have similar lifestyles as well as similar values and beliefs around money.

Quite often our financial comfort zones are based on the way we grow up. Suppose, for example, Serena's parents just barely earned enough to pay the bills and she grew up in an atmosphere of constant worry about money. She got a college education, thanks to a scholarship, and went on to build a successful accounting business. Yet, despite her substantial income, she still lived in a small apartment, drove a ten-year-old car, and believed she "couldn't afford" to travel or get regular tickets to the symphony. She was still living within the financial boundaries she learned from her family.

At the opposite extreme, suppose Diane's parents had so much inherited wealth that they essentially had no upper limits on what they could spend. As a little girl, she learned that a "normal" lifestyle included trips to Paris to buy school clothes, birthday celebrations featuring world-famous entertainers, and taking the family jet across the country as routinely as other kids might take the subway across town. As an adult, with a generous but not unlimited income from her own trust fund, Diane had no idea how to manage. She was constantly running out of money and going to her parents for more. She was unable to adjust to a lower financial comfort zone than the one she knew growing up.

Living at the lower end of your financial comfort zone means choosing to impose limits on your family spending even though your income doesn't require those limits. Here are a few examples:

- Owning a vacation home in Vail, but one that is relatively modest.

- Traveling all over the world but not isolating yourselves in luxury resorts.
- Driving ordinary vehicles rather than iconic luxury brands.
- Taking care of your own personal needs and expecting your kids to do the same. You may not do your own laundry or take care of the yard and garden, but you can clean your own bathroom, pick up after yourself, and do chores around the house.
- Living in an upper-middle-class neighborhood rather than an exclusive gated community.
- Sending your kids to public schools or local private schools rather than exclusive boarding schools.

The point of living within your means isn't the level of your lifestyle or the amount of your spending. A lifestyle that includes international travel, second homes, and private planes may be pushing the upper limits of one family's financial comfort zone but may be at the lower end for another family. What matters most is choosing to live within limits. This helps kids learn that living well doesn't necessarily mean spending the most or being "at the top," but that there is far more satisfaction in enjoying what you have and using it well.

On the other hand, "not acting like rich folks" doesn't mean making a pretense of poverty. Pretending you can't afford to spend money that you clearly have is just another form of dysfunction around wealth. Denying that you have wealth is the opposite of believing wealth gives you the right to do whatever you want. Neither extreme shows an empowered relationship with money.

I've worked with parents who talk openly with their kids about their distaste for blatant consumerism and their choice to live a modest lifestyle. This is not the same as claiming "we can't afford it." Setting limits based on pretended poverty is just as bad as setting no limits, because kids know you aren't being truthful.

Instead, you can say, "we choose not to spend our money that way," or "that isn't worth the money to us." If you can easily afford to do or buy whatever you want, it isn't reasonable to say yes or no to kids simply in terms of cost. It's more useful to talk about whether spending x amount of dollars on y product or z experience will give you value for the money you spend.

Communicating Openly About Money

One evening, when my daughter was in about third grade, she came over to see what I was doing when I was paying household bills. She saw the check I was writing for the car payment, and she was shocked at the amount. It probably hadn't occurred to her before that we had to make payments for the car. We spent about four or five minutes in conversation about borrowing, paying bills, and the family budget. In those few minutes, she learned a lot, not just about budgeting and our family's income and expenses, but about money in general.

That time with my daughter was a good example of taking advantage of a teachable moment. This is one of the most effective ways we as parents can communicate with our kids about money. There certainly can be value in setting aside specific times to talk with them about the family wealth, giving, family businesses, and so on. But when we as parents are open to answering kids' questions or talking about money matters when they initiate the conversation, we can be more confident of having their interest and attention. A few minutes of teaching when children are engaged can be more valuable than an hour spent when they are only half paying attention.

Taking advantage of teachable moments requires parents to be willing to talk about money in general and the family money in particular. That willingness may well be the hardest part of the whole process. In our society, money is largely a taboo subject.

It's right up there with—or even ahead of—politics, religion, and sex. We're taught that polite people don't ask how much money others have, earn, or spend. Many companies discourage employees from revealing their salaries to each other. Even close friends and family members tend not to discuss money in any detail. We're accustomed to being private and even secretive about money.

In wealthy families, talking about money can be even more difficult than it is in middle-class families. In some cases, money may be almost "invisible," for several reasons. When there is plenty of money for whatever the family needs, it is less of a day-to-day concern. Kids are less likely to hear conversations about whether the family can afford a vacation trip to Disney World or whether it's time to replace a car or the furnace. If accountants or assistants take care of the actual bill-paying, kids don't have an opportunity to ask money questions when they see parents writing out monthly checks. If a housekeeper does the shopping, kids aren't following Mom or Dad down the aisles in the supermarket watching them buy meat or produce based on the weekly specials.

Another factor that encourages money secrecy in wealthy families is a reluctance to expose oneself to the envy or resentment of those outside the family. This lesson is one that some kids from wealthy families learn early and painfully. When an elementary school teacher asks a class, "What did you get for Christmas?" it doesn't take long for a kid to figure out that his family's safari trip to Africa isn't in the same category as other kids' Legos and video games. One man described the discomfort of returning to school after the winter holiday when he was about 12 or 13. The teacher asked the kids to share with the class their favorite gifts. This young man got increasingly nervous as his turn approached because it was obvious that his gifts were far larger than anyone else's in the class. In a desperate attempt to fit in, he said his favorite gift was underwear. In retrospect the story was humorous, but at the time it was quite painful. It represented his sense of not fitting in and being judged as a rich kid who had everything handed to him.

It's helpful in wealthy families to have conversations with kids about the difference between privacy and secrecy. Privacy is keeping within the family information that is no one else's business. Secrecy is a conspiracy of silence both inside and outside the family. Talking about money is taboo, and wealth becomes the elephant in the living room that no one acknowledges. Secrecy fosters a sense of guilt or shame about the family wealth. To avoid a pattern of secrecy, I encourage families to communicate openly about money with each other. Parents can take advantage of opportunities to talk about money and teach their kids how to spend, save, and give it in healthy ways.

I sometimes equate this with having healthy communication about any difficult issue in the family. For example, if a family has a child with learning difficulties, they certainly wouldn't want to hide that fact. At the same time, there would be no need to share details of the child's struggles or accomplishments with everyone outside the family. That would violate the child's privacy. Instead, the family members would need to become aware that there are different layers of trust with different people. There are some people outside the family who can be trusted with intimate information, but it's important to be selective and have healthy boundaries with assessing who can be trusted. In the same way, details about the family money can be safely shared with certain outsiders and don't need to be discussed with others.

Intentionality and Teaching by Example

"What you do speaks so loud that I cannot hear what you say."

Ralph Waldo Emerson

As with so many other aspects of parenting, the most important tool for teaching children about money is example. Parents in flourishing wealthy families are consciously aware of the values they convey. They do their best to live those values from day to day. They model stewardship, responsibility, and restraint in their own lives.

At the same time, they understand the importance of intentional teaching. In legacy families that are successful in transferring wealth in healthy ways, parents take an active role in teaching children how to manage wealth responsibly. They don't take for granted that growing up with wealth means children will learn how to live comfortably with money. They see the necessity for consciously helping their children build empowered relationships with money. As one couple said when they first hired me, "We don't quite understand what you do, but we do understand that it's time we deliberately used for our family some of the same planning strategies and sense of mission we've used in building our business."

Intentional financial parenting requires time, effort, and attention. It also requires the flexibility and knowledge to teach kids in ways that are appropriate to their ages and their individual needs. Some of the components of strong financial parenting are:

- Building a healthy, empowered relationship with money yourself.
- Taking advantage of opportunities to teach children basic money skills.
- Setting an example of gratitude, appreciation, and restraint.
- Teaching kids how to guard against resentment, envy, and false "friends" who will exploit them for what they have rather than enjoy them for who they are.
- Understanding that emotional support and financial support are often not the same thing.
- Involving kids in the family's social mission.

Financial parenting is just one of many challenges that make being a parent so difficult. Yet, when we see kids developing their abilities, making responsible choices about their money, and giving back with genuine gratitude, it's worth every bit of effort we give to it.

Over the years, I have worked with many successful people who have accomplished a great deal. They have built businesses from scratch, been inventors and innovators, used their talents in significant ways, and been recognized as leaders in their careers and their communities. Yet when I talk with them, they often say something similar to this: "What I take the most pride in in my life is my family. Being a parent is the most difficult and most important thing I do. It's also one of the most rewarding."

CHAPTER FIVE

FINANCIAL PARENTING STRATEGIES

HELPING KIDS DEVELOP empowered relationships with money requires time, effort, and intentionality. The first and probably the most difficult step toward effective financial parenting is making the choice to do it. Deciding to take on the challenge, however, doesn't magically give you the necessary skills the job demands. This chapter describes some of the strategies parents have used successfully in teaching young children about money.

Teach Basic Money Skills

The basics of money can be broken down into four components: Earn, Save, Spend, and Share.

Earn. This is the piece that is all too easy to miss in wealthy families. For one thing, members of later generations are often disconnected from earning the family money. It's just "there." As discussed in Chapter Three, it's important to connect kids with the source of the income that provides for them. It's also essential for kids to understand early that money and earning go together. From time to time I see wealthy families where kids graduate from college without ever having held any kind of a job. They may have good academic records, but without the experience of working, preferably outside the family, they are ill-equipped to start out in their chosen careers.

With young children, a common issue is whether they should be expected to earn their allowances. Different families have different ideas about whether allowances should be tied to chores or other requirements like keeping rooms clean. My own belief is that allowances are a great idea, and they should be separate from chores. Everyone shares in the benefit of receiving allowances because they are members of the family. In the same way, everyone shares in the responsibility of doing chores because they are members of the family. Both Mom and Dad have jobs outside the family, and they do chores without being paid. Kids' jobs are school and activities, and they also do chores without being paid.

At the same time, it can be great to have extra tasks for kids that they do get paid for. This gives them the opportunity at a young age to learn the early lessons of saving for that special big-ticket item and the satisfaction derived from earning. For example, I used to hire my children to clean my in-home office and wash my car. Generally, it's best to hire kids for chores that are seasonal, like raking leaves, or that are not part of the everyday tasks of keeping the household running smoothly.

Both paying kids for work they do and rewarding them financially for behavior or achievements like getting good grades are techniques to use with some caution. In either case, it's important not to overuse payment or rewards. The last thing you want is for kids to start thinking they ought to be paid for activities that are an everyday part of their responsibilities. Payment amounts for small jobs or extra chores also should be reasonable in proportion to the work that kids do. You don't want to create little mega-capitalists who learn to value their work according to a grossly inflated pay scale.

Save. In many families, kids are required to save part of their allowances. A method I like is to give each child three containers.

Clear jars work well, because kids can easily see how much they accumulate. Then establish a tradition of distributing allowances at a given time each week, and have kids put their money into the jars. A designated amount, say ten percent, goes into the "saving" jar.

Some families also require kids to save a portion of any money they earn or receive as gifts. It's a good idea, as well, to teach kids about saving for short-term and long-term goals. Short-term saving is to accumulate money for something small like a new video game. Long-term saving is to accumulate money for larger goals like their first iPhone or a special experience.

Carly, at 12, was an aspiring cellist who played in the school orchestra, took private lessons, and had been accepted into a junior symphony. Her teacher recommended a three-week summer music camp. Even though her parents could easily have afforded the camp fee, they chose to require Carly to pay half. For three months, she saved the majority of her allowance and earned extra money by walking friends' dogs. When it was time to register for the camp, she proudly handed over her half of the tuition.

When young kids accumulate some savings in their jars or piggy banks, then the next step is to help them open their own savings accounts. Don't stop there—show them how to read the statements so they can watch their savings accumulate.

As kids get older, many families give them small amounts to invest as a hands-on way of teaching them about business and economics. Both the amounts involved and the level of education about investing can increase as the kids become teenagers and young adults. One important piece of this learning is to give them a chance to make their own mistakes while the amounts are relatively small. The challenge for us as parents is to strike a balance between providing information and support and yet letting them find their own way.

Share. If you use a three-jar system for allowances, another ten percent or so goes in the "sharing" jar. This could be used for church giving, charitable donations, and family gifts such as Christmas and birthday presents. In my family, we allowed the kids to decide where to give, but as they got older we expected them to research causes they wanted to give to.

Spend. The rest of the allowance goes into the "spending" jar, and that is the amount kids get to use for the things they want to buy. Here is where things can get tricky. Some parents allow kids to spend their "lifestyle money" in any way they want. Others set limits—no buying video games, maybe, or not more than a set amount per week on junk food. Neither approach is right or wrong; what matters most is to let kids make some of their own money decisions and experience the consequences—both good and bad—of those decisions.

No matter what method you use to teach kids about saving and spending, it's essential to be clear up front about what you will pay for and what they need to pay for. The rules will need to evolve as kids get older, of course, but it's important to apply them consistently while they are in force. Don't sabotage yourself and confuse the kids by setting limits and then disregarding them.

Let Kids Experience Consequences

It's not in kids' best interests to allow them to be "too rich to fail." Instead, give them the gift of allowing them to make their own mistakes and experience the consequences.

This is among the hardest things for any parents to do. No one wants to be the mean, heartless parent who allows a poor child to suffer. Yet if we want our children to grow up to be responsible adults, it's crucial to allow them to learn from small mistakes before they're in a position to make big mistakes. Don't buy your kids out of trouble. This kind of parenting is hard.

Enforcing limits and allowing consequences takes effort, commitment, and overcoming our own need to rescue our babies. It can be especially challenging in wealthy families, because the means are there and it would be so much easier just to pay the bill and forget about it.

It's essential, however, to respect children enough to let them suffer their own consequences while the stakes are still minor. Letting them experience small amounts of pain from inconsequential childhood mistakes will save them from larger pain and serious consequences later.

Here are a few of the ways to let kids experience consequences. Not all of them are specifically financial, but non-monetary consequences are as important as financial ones when it comes to teaching responsible behavior.

a. If they break something because they are being rowdy or careless or deliberately destructive, they pay for it. Of course, this is assuming that your house is kid-friendly enough that they can be normal, active children without the risk of breaking expensive stuff every time they gallop into a room. Yes, kids can and should learn to be careful with valuable belongings. But if a four-year-old damages a priceless collectible because it wasn't protected, that is more the parents' fault than the child's.

b. If they make a commitment, they keep it. If you've made a deal with Ethan that you'll take him somewhere after he cleans his room, be sure his half of the bargain is carried out before you implement yours. As with so many other aspects of parenting, the most important way of teaching this behavior is through example. Keeping promises we make to our children is the clearest way for them to learn to keep promises of their own.

c. I worked with a family that had education as a core value. They let their children know they would pay all expenses related to a college education for 4.5 years, including spending money so they wouldn't be required to work when in college. This arrangement worked well for the first two children, but when the third, Elizabeth, started college she went through her spending allowance in the first month. The parents could easily have transferred more money to her account, but decided instead to let her experience the natural consequences for breaking her agreement. She had to get a part-time job. Interestingly, the following semesters Elizabeth didn't overspend, but she also choose to continue working because she enjoyed the sense of autonomy it gave her.

d. One of the most fundamental lessons to teach children is that when a given amount of money is gone, it's gone. Don't violate your own limits by lending or giving them more after you've said this is all they get. It's a good idea to enforce this limit when kids are young. If Allison blows her vacation money on cheap junk in the first two days, let her look wistfully at souvenirs or treats she can't buy for the rest of the trip. Learning this lesson early may help kids avoid experiences like Elizabeth's college over-spending where the consequences are more severe.

What I learned to use with my own kids was a phrase that might be dated but that I found very useful. When they came to me with a sad story about not having any money left, I would say, "Gee, that's a bummer." When you respond in this way, you agree that there is a problem but you don't jump in to fix it. You let the child learn the lesson.

Now, this isn't easy. It's very hard to look a pleading child in the eye and refuse to bail her out with 20 bucks you would never miss. Especially for wealthy parents, it's easier to buy kids out of trouble than to stand back and do nothing. As parents, we need to remind ourselves constantly that this kind of tough love is in our kids' best interests. This is one case where the cliché of "this hurts me worse than it hurts you" is probably true.

e. One challenge in wealthy families is deciding how much allowance kids should get. It's not reasonable or appropriate to create a sense of pseudo-poverty by limiting kids to five bucks a week when the family budget and lifestyle would support a much larger amount. This isn't likely to teach kids anything except resentment. At the same time, it can be destructive to provide allowances that are so large the kids don't have the chance to learn to limit their spending. Most successful families seem to set allowances in the lower range of what is "normal" among their kids' peers. If in doubt, less rather than more is probably better. It's also important to be clear about what kids are expected to provide for themselves out of their allowances. Some families, for example, give teenagers a monthly or quarterly clothing allowance as a way of helping them learn to shop and manage their money.

f. In setting limits and allowing children to learn from their mistakes, it is crucial for parents to work together. Suppose Mom has told Allison it's too bad she spent all her vacation money but she isn't giving her any more. Then Dad slips her an extra $20 and says, "Don't tell Mom." This teaches Allison two destructive lessons. One is that rules don't really apply to her because someone will bail her out in spite of them. The other is that she can manipulate her parents and play one against the other.

Don't Give Carelessly or Destructively

One young mother from the fourth generation in a wealthy family had this question: "How do I help my children keep their innocence when everyone knows about the family money? Their grandmother is flying my little boy and seven of his friends to Disney World for his eighth birthday party."

The solution is simple enough: don't give too much, and don't give too soon. Give consciously and deliberately with the child's best interests in mind. Of course, just because it's simple doesn't mean it's easy. Choosing to limit your giving—and to limit giving by other members of the family—can be a challenge. Here are some suggestions that other families have used successfully:

a. Think before you give. Consider the child's comfort and needs rather than what you might think of as "the best."

An entrepreneur whose successful business had created significant wealth celebrated his son's 16th birthday with the gift of a new car—a gleaming white Lincoln Continental. There's nothing wrong with buying a 16-year-old a new car. But this man didn't stop to think about what kind of car would be appropriate for a teenager. The Lincoln probably represented the father's idea of top-of-the-line value. He didn't consider that his son might not share that view. He didn't realize that his son would be mortified to drive to school in an ostentatious vehicle labeled the "Pimpmobile" by his friends."

b. Avoid giving in ways that set children apart. You want their money experiences to be as normal as possible, which in an affluent family can be difficult.

Many kids today would see a family vacation trip to Disney World as "normal" even if their own family couldn't afford it. A quick flight there in the family jet for a birthday party, when the average kid might get to take a few friends to a skating rink, is something else again. This kind of high-profile spending may be well-intentioned, but the result can be destructive. Instead of making enjoyable memories, it can make children's lives harder by setting them up to be envied and resented by their peers.

One third-generation daughter-in-law who had done an excellent job with her young daughters told me she was concerned because the matriarch in the family had offered to take her and her first grade daughter to New York to shop as a gift for the little girl's birthday. To make matters more complicated, they would be taking the private plane. With tears streaming down her face, this young mother told me, "I can't compete with that. What will my daughter expect for her next birthday, with the bar set so high?" Gifts like these can establish an almost surreal level of expectation that could plant seeds of entitlement. In our conversation, the daughter-in-law decided she and her husband would thank the grandmother for her incredible generosity but respectfully decline her offer.

c. Don't give money as a substitute for time. It's become almost a cliché: the busy parent who doesn't have time to shop for a birthday gift or attend a special school performance, but tries to compensate by sending the child off to the mall with a hundred-dollar bill or a credit card. A pattern of giving money or things because we're "too busy" to spend time with our children teaches them several negative lessons. First, work and other activities are more important than people. Second, money and possessions are substitutes for relationships. Third, people can be "bought off" with money instead of time and attention.

The way we bond with our kids, get to know who they are and what matters to them, and pass on our values is through spending time with them. This doesn't have to take the form of trips, big events, or long blocks of daily time, either. Parents learn to take advantage of brief opportunities throughout the day, in much the same way they can take advantage of teachable moments to pass on information. Memories and close relationships are built through small interactions and shared moments: conversations at the dinner table or in the car on the way to school, bedtime rituals like reading stories, and working together on projects or chores. Delegating too much of the routine of raising children to others deprives both parents and children of these opportunities.

As parents, nothing we can buy for or give to our kids is more important than our time. Remember that "love" is rarely spelled M-O-N-E-Y, but is often spelled T-I-M-E and sometimes spelled N-O.

d. Don't give in ways that foster helplessness. A young father was watching his six-month-old daughter wobble on her elbows and knees as she struggled to get to a toy just out of reach. He said, "I've noticed that she really learns things when she gets mad. She works harder. Just watch—she's going to be crawling any minute now."

This goes back to the idea of optimal frustration. Children learn competence by working to solve problems and struggling to overcome obstacles. Giving too much or too quickly teaches them to rely on outside intervention instead of their own abilities. It encourages them to think of themselves as helpless or incapable. What parents see as financial and emotional support is sometimes the opposite, because it interferes with children's responsibility and opportunity to learn to take care of themselves.

Giving in ways that interfere with competence can take many forms. A few examples are hovering over a baby to hand her a toy the instant she wants it, buying all of your daughter's Girl Scout cookies instead of helping her figure out how to sell them, or buying an expensive racing bike for your son when he expresses a casual interest in competitive cycling instead of waiting to see whether his interest is genuine.

e. Set limits for others' giving to your children. Much of the time, this means saying no to your own parents, which is even harder than saying no to your kids. A common dynamic I see in families is first-generation wealthy grandparents expressing frustration and worry that the values of hard work and frugality which helped them succeed are not being learned by their grandchildren. At the same time, the grandparents may be buying the grandkids lavish gifts, taking them on expensive trips, and giving them money over and above the allowances set by their parents. Generation Two, caught in the middle, has the unenviable task of trying to say no in both directions at once. This is especially hard if they are themselves dependent on their parents' financial support.

Here are some ways that thriving families deal with this challenge:

- Talk to the grandparents to help them see the harmful side of their generosity. Enlist their help and support rather than being confrontational.
- Encourage grandparents to look back and talk about the lessons they learned from their own struggles.
- Usually it's best for these conversations to be led by the son or daughter rather than the daughter-in-law or son-in-law.
- Take a hard look at the example you are setting for your children. Are you financially dependent on your parents? Do you accept lavish gifts that make you uncomfortable?
- Don't scold children for accepting gifts when the real problem is the grandparents who are giving them.
- Find ways to encourage and allow grandparents to be generous and giving in appropriate ways. The key may be to work together to find ways for them to give time and mentoring more than money.

- Grandparents need to honor the boundaries of their children and communicate with the parents directly instead of going through their grandchildren.

Teach Kids to Give

Many families require kids to give a portion of their allowances to churches or charities. For giving that provides a stronger emotional impact, some families also involve kids in what I call giving from the "emotional checkbook" instead of the financial one. One of my family's most memorable experiences, when our kids were teenagers, was a trip to help with a building project for an orphanage in Mexico. For a week, we spent long days doing hard physical work. We didn't have any time for traditional "fun" vacation activities, and we ate the same frugal meals the children in the orphanage had. At the end of the trip the kids all said this had been the best vacation of their lives. One of them suggested giving up our family Christmas celebration and donating the money to the orphanage instead.

There are many ways to give and many worthwhile causes to give to. What is most important is to involve children in the family's social mission. As always, the most important teaching is done by example. Talk openly about values the family stands for as well as your personal beliefs about giving back and living with purpose. Let children see what and how you give. Encourage them to develop their own individual values and give in their own ways.

Live a "Normal" Life

Several clients have told me that building success and wealth relatively slowly and remaining "under the radar" makes life easier. Kids who grow up with enough money to live well and enjoy opportunities, but who don't see the family as "rich," tend to function more comfortably in the world than those whose parents achieve sudden or conspicuous wealth.

Staying "under the radar" can also be done successfully for later generations who are born into wealth. Even parents whose careers are very public can choose to protect their children from the limelight. There are prominent Hollywood actors, for example, whose success depends to some degree on being visible, yet who still manage quite successfully to keep their private lives out of the media.

Here are a few ways that successful families manage to live "normal" lives:

a. Teach children basic life skills and responsibilities. Even if kids don't have to vacuum under their own beds and scrub their own toilets, require them to keep their own rooms neat and pick up after themselves. Thriving families don't let kids learn that it's someone else's responsibility to clean up their messes. Let them learn to cook and do routine household chores, expect them to take care of their pets themselves, and teach them by example that they aren't too special to have to do the same things everyone else does.

b. If you have household employees, whether it's a weekly housecleaner or a full live-in staff, be clear to both your children and your employees that the staff members work for you, not your kids. Establish an environment where kids with wealth are outranked by adults without it. Expect your children to treat all adults with respect and to regard their parents' employees as authority figures rather than subordinates. Teach and expect your kids to make polite requests, not give orders. Make clear to staff members that they have your support in saying no if those polite requests are unreasonable, violate house rules, or interfere with their work. Give your staff members that authority, and back them up when they use it.

At the same time, allow kids to see that managing household employees carries responsibilities similar to those of running a small business. They will learn about hiring, supervising, and working with people from the model they live with at home.

c. Make your house a home meant to be lived in rather than a showplace meant to be looked at. Have areas where kids can do messy art or science projects, hang out with friends, get dirty, not worry about breaking expensive furnishings, and be ordinary. Choose furnishings for kids' rooms based more on utility and their taste than on cost or appearance. Let them do their own decorating. One man was a young teenager when his parents built a distinctive house designed by a famous architect. He was embarrassed by the house and hated the attention it generated. It wasn't a home to him, but an all-too-public symbol of his family's new wealth that set him apart from other kids.

d. Define "quality" in ways to meet your children's needs. Don't automatically choose schools, summer camps, or activities for your kids because they're supposed to be "the best" or assume that the most expensive will provide the most value. Take the time to investigate and make sure a particular program is right for your kids.

e. Involve kids with people in different financial circumstances. A family philosophy of connectedness with people in various financial circumstances can help children learn to be comfortable with those who live differently than their own families do. These connections might come through church, public schools, or activities and organizations.

Volunteering through church projects or youth groups to work with people in poverty can certainly be worthwhile. Yet if this is the only interaction kids have with people without money, it has the potential to be negative. If the primary way they see low-income people is as victims or those who need help, the interaction can almost be a form of "slumming." It can emphasize people's differences based on income instead of focusing on their similarities.

f. Help kids find places to be anonymous. A fundamental aspect of 12-Step recovery programs like Alcoholics Anonymous is not revealing members' identities. People initially introduce themselves by first names only. One important reason for this is to protect people's privacy. A second and equally important benefit, however, is to remove the superficial labels that define us to each other. Members of a group relate to each other as fellow human beings helping each other cope with similar challenges. They get to know one another as simply "Jack" or "Sara" or "Andy," instead of first as a banker, sales clerk, construction worker, stay-at-home mom, or millionaire.

Children from wealthy families can benefit from environments that foster a similar kind of anonymity. Experiences like summer camps that focus on art, music, science, or other specific interests can provide places for kids to spend time with others who are their peers based on abilities and interests rather than financial status.

g. Use the gift of time that wealth can give you. One of the benefits wealth can provide is choices about how you use your time, including the opportunity to spend more time with your children.

h. Provide kids with experiences rather than things. I've seen wealthy families who choose to live in upper-middle-class areas and send their kids to public schools. At the same time, they travel extensively all over the world, install telescopes in their back yards, or take the children to operas or to the Olympics or on archeological digs. They use their wealth intentionally, not to live a generically lavish lifestyle, but to pursue the family's interests and live according to the family's values.

Provide Responsibilities and Challenges

There is a reason that the "hero's journey," where a young person is faced with challenges and learns to overcome them, is such an integral part of folk tales and traditions in so many cultures. Some type of struggle is an essential component of maturing into a competent adult. A life that is too easy is disempowering. It takes away people's opportunity to develop a work ethic and learn to trust their own ability to solve problems.

In wealthy families, where there is no need to overcome financial challenges, it's important for parents to provide opportunities that challenge children in other ways. One fundamental way is to expect them to do the work related to their responsibilities themselves, instead of paying someone else to do it. The SAT cheating scandal that came to light in New York in 2011, where high school students were hiring other students to take the test for them, is a glaring example of what can happen when kids are allowed to learn to buy the illusion of success instead of working for their own achievements.

Susan Bradley, author of *Sudden Money*, described an incident at one of her Money Camps, designed to teach teenagers about money. In one activity, the students were asked to guess what the Dow Jones average would be on a given day. At the end of the week, prizes were given for the closest guesses. The very wealthy and powerful father of one of the students called Susan the next week to complain that his son had the closest guess but didn't get a prize. She told him, "I didn't count your son's entry because that wasn't his number, it was yours. I saw you give it to him."

The father was irate. He told her that all the parents had probably given their kids the answer. To him, assuming parents should use their resources to smooth the path for their children was normal. He didn't understand that his help for his son was actually harmful in the long term.

When we allow kids to solve their own problems, we are teaching them to trust their own abilities. Instead of giving them solutions, it's often more useful to ask questions like, "What do you think might work?" From the time kids are small, we can practice treating them as whole, capable human beings who need help and support from time to time but who are able to find their own way. This teaches children an essential and empowering message: "I trust you with your life." When we as parents trust our kids, they will learn to trust themselves.

Help Kids Cope with Envy and Resentment

Consider the phenomenal social changes that have been made in the last 30 years. It is no longer acceptable to openly discriminate against people because of their skin color, gender, heritage, or sexual orientation. About the only group that it is "acceptable" to discriminate against is rich people. If we hear a rich person talk about the burden of wealth or struggles, we roll our collective eyes and respond, *what a nice problem to have.*

Wealthy kids know they are targets of envy and resentment. They want what all kids want, which is just to be accepted for who they are. I have worked with numerous young adults from wealthy families who describe the pain of being regarded as just a stuck-up rich kid. Often a family meeting is the first time that many of them speak up and share what it was like growing up wealthy. They often have felt isolated and too embarrassed to tell anyone how they were feeling. Often when they do speak up in the family meeting about the pain, they are met with support from siblings or cousins who proclaim, "Me too!" Meanwhile, the parents, hearing about this for the first time, are wondering out loud, "I wish we had known. What could we have done? What can we do now?"

One young woman in particular sobbed as she described what it was like growing up the target of envy and resentment. Her father was a well-known businessman and CEO of a public company. She came from a loving family, but she spent most of her childhood not knowing who among her peer group to trust because of comments made behind her back that she was just a "rich bitch." It made her suspicious of her peer group's motives, and she had several instances of public humiliation directed at her because of her family name. She just wanted to be related to as a normal kid with typical struggles, but she was never able to free herself of the stigma of her family wealth.

These types of conversations are part of what makes family meetings so valuable. Each member is able to openly discuss the formerly taboo subjects that they have been carrying for years. They can receive support from the people in their lives who are uniquely qualified to offer that support and understanding.

Teach by Example

When I meet with a new client family for the first time, it's rare to have a family member pick me up at the airport. Many times a car will be sent for me, or else I make my own arrangements for a cab to the hotel. One couple, however, not only picked me up themselves but did so in a used Honda Accord.

This family was very intentional about living ordinary, inconspicuous lives that were congruent with their values of modesty, frugality, stewardship, and giving back. Although they traveled regularly and encouraged their children to take advantage of a wide variety of educational opportunities, they lived in an ordinary upper-middle-class neighborhood and sent their kids to public schools. They talked openly with their kids about their scorn for thoughtless consumerism and were very willing to say no to what they considered unreasonable or inappropriate spending. They did not pretend to be poor, but they were direct in teaching the children their belief that money was not to be spent carelessly but in ways that provided value in return.

Other successful families choose to live much more lavish lifestyles but still model strong values of using their wealth consciously and respectfully. They make deliberate choices about what is worthwhile to spend money on and what is not, and they include their children in conversations about those choices. They also set a strong example of treating others around them with courtesy and respect. I've seen wealthy and powerful business owners who treat all their employees as honored and valued partners and give them most of the credit for the success of the business. They also tend to treat food servers and household employees with the same courtesy they extend to their financial equals. Modeling attitudes like this, at work and at home, is the single most effective way to teach children that having money isn't a justification for disrespectful or bullying behavior.

Modeling an attitude of appreciation is also common in flourishing families. Members of these families routinely express their gratitude for what they have. This isn't smugness or arrogance, but an attitude of humility and an awareness of having been blessed. It goes hand in hand with a sense of responsibility and stewardship. These parents and grandparents live in a way that might be expressed as, "No matter how much wealth we have, we can all benefit from approaching our precious lives with a daily sense of gratitude."

Members of thriving families also realize that having money

doesn't automatically confer the knowledge to use it well or teach children to do the same. They are willing to take advantage of learning opportunities in order to build the skills they want to pass on to their children. Parents who want their kids to grow up to have empowered relationships with money understand the need to first create such relationships for themselves.

CHAPTER SIX
PREPARING HEIRS

A NUMBER OF years ago I was talking with my Uncle Frank, the owner with his wife of a very successful independent insurance company. Their son worked in the business; their daughter didn't. I asked him about his succession plan. He laughed and said, "Oh, I'm going to do my estate planning on the golf course."

I asked what he meant by that, and he said, "Someday I'll have a heart attack on the 18th green, and I'll just let them figure it out."

As estate planning strategies go, this isn't exactly one to recommend. But the temptation to just "let them figure it out" is there for all of us. We're reluctant to sit down with family members and talk about all these things. In some families more than others, the whole area of estate planning is riddled with possible land mines along the way. It's not an easy area to address for anyone.

The crucial element that is missing in my uncle's approach to estate planning is *intentionality*. In flourishing wealthy families, the older generations think in terms of "legacy planning." They realize it involves much more than making decisions about who gets how much of the family money. They understand the importance of preparing heirs to take over the responsibility of the wealth. They look beyond the question of "What do we leave to them?" and think in terms of "How do we help them be successful with what they will inherit?" They create estate plans that don't "talk at" heirs, but "talk to" them.

A second element that is especially important in legacy planning for wealthy families is the idea of *stewardship*. Families dealing with inherited wealth no longer have the luxury of simply saying, "It's my money and I can do whatever I want with it." In thriving families, succeeding generations tend to see themselves as the stewards or custodians of the money. They have the responsibility to manage it well not just for themselves, but also on behalf of future generations.

Ideally, intentionally preparing heirs for the responsibilities they will inherit begins with effective financial parenting when kids are young. It's also possible to do a good job of preparing heirs even if that early foundation hasn't been as strong as parents would have liked it to be. I've worked with families in both circumstances and have seen them succeed. This chapter covers some of the elements they have found important.

Encourage Children To Grow Up and Separate from the Family

One of the most important tasks of growing up for teenagers is to separate from Mom and Dad. One of the hardest tasks of parenting is for Mom and Dad to let them go. This transition is hard in any family, but wealth complicates it.

It's ironic that having a great deal of money, which we sometimes describe as financial independence, can actually foster dependence. One example of this is the stereotype of the "trust fund babies" who are kept in a dependent position by having to justify their choices and lifestyle in order to withdraw funds. Sometimes older generations, wanting to pass along important core values like hard work and stewardship, may try to do so by giving money with so many strings attached that younger generations are kept in a childish position.

Even in families that work hard not to use money to manip-ulate and control, having wealth can make it harder for young people to separate from their parents and the family. In today's world, an extended adolescence or "emerging adult" stage for people in their 20s is increasingly common. Young people are marrying later, and it's more common for college graduates to come home to live with parents for a time.

In wealthy families, the emerging adult stage can be a strong benefit if it's used intentionally. A gap year between high school and college, for example, can offer strong learning opportunities such as travel, exploring career possibilities, and volunteering. Young people who don't need to earn their way through college have the chance to participate fully in extracurricular activities and other important aspects of college life.

At the same time, when financial need isn't a strong factor in the drive to grow up and become self-sufficient, it's possible to extend this emerging adult stage more or less indefinitely. Parents in thriving families don't allow this to happen, but are intentional about supporting their kids in moving into full adulthood.

As young people grow up and build their own adult lives, both children and parents in most families figure out a com-fortable "optimal distance" that maintains family closeness but allows younger generations the space to be themselves. This dis-tance varies from family to family: some kids and parents might touch base by phone or email almost daily and have family gath-erings every few weeks. Others might be comfortable with occa-sional phone calls or emails and seeing each other perhaps once a year.

A typical extended middle-class family whose members are close might get together several times a year. Yet they don't share ownership of a business, the grandparents aren't provid-ing allowances or trust funds to children and grandchildren, and there isn't a joint pool of family money or a charitable foundation to be managed. Money isn't something people really need to talk about. It isn't necessarily one of the points of connection within the family.

Members of wealthy legacy families, on the other hand, are more enmeshed financially regardless of how close they may be emotionally. They may be sharing family businesses, assets, trusts, and foundations. A certain level of communication and connection is simply required, regardless of the degree of closeness that various family members might prefer. They have less choice over maintaining a comfortable optimal distance. This makes it even more essential for parents to help kids make the transition into emotional independence.

Prepare Heirs Both Emotionally and Intellectually

In all the families I've worked with, I continue to be impressed by how important it is to prepare heirs emotionally. Let's look at the Woods family as an example. The three daughters and one son, in their late 30s and 40s, are eventually going to inherit around 50 or 60 million dollars apiece. This is something they've known about for a number of years. As the second generation, they grew up with the wealth, so this is nothing particularly new to them.

A financial advisor brought me in to consult with the Woods family when the parents started working on a detailed estate plan, because the second generation was experiencing such emotional difficulties. Even though they knew theoretically about the money, there was something about the reality of seeing the numbers and discussing the inheritance that left them off balance. It was a shock to the system. My role with the family was to help them process that shock and move forward.

One question I'm sometimes asked is, "When is the best time to give kids the numbers? At what age are they ready to know the details of the family's net worth?"

Of course, there isn't a single right answer to this question. I do think knowing the numbers is important. In today's Internet world, any kids old enough to use a computer can probably get online and get at least a rough idea of the family's wealth, which is one more reason not to wait too long to share that information. What's important is to help kids avoid the shock of learning details of the family finances before they are emotionally prepared.

Even for members of third, fourth, and later generations, who take the family wealth for granted, the prospect of a large inheritance can bring more fear than joy. Parents, and families as a whole, need to keep two important questions in mind: "How is inheriting this wealth going to feel to you emotionally?" and "How can we help you get prepared for it?"

Certainly, one way to help prepare heirs emotionally is to make sure they're prepared intellectually. A basic education in how money works is essential. It's surprising how many kids in wealthy families grow up without that education. The money provides some insulation or protection from life that can limit their learning and growth around finances, unless parents are very intentional about teaching them what they need to know.

Money knowledge alone, however, isn't enough to prepare heirs for the responsibilities of wealth. One of my important roles with my client families is facilitating conversations about the emotional impact of having money. This gives younger family members a chance to talk about their fears, their doubts, and their expectations. It also provides a place for older family members to share their own experiences around inheriting or building wealth. These conversations are most helpful when they don't focus on "This is what you should do," but on "This is what it was/is like for me." When older generations can talk openly and honestly about the challenges, responsibilities, and benefits of wealth, they allow younger generations to learn from their experiences.

One of my interviews for this book was with Jim, a third-generation farmer whose father had defaulted to "equal but not fair" in the estate planning between his two sons. Jim had worked on the family farm his whole life, while his brother decided to leave the small community and explore another career. When the father made his estate plan, he wanted to avoid any conflict or feelings of one son being treated better than the other, so he divided the farm in half to give each brother an equal share. Unfortunately, the two brothers ended up in litigation over the "fairness" of the estate plan. Because of this experience, Jim didn't want to make the same mistake with his children. He used the story to frame the importance of talking openly about issues and to emphasize the importance in his immediate family of discussing the issue of what was fair and equal.

In many of my interviews, various family members mentioned that one of the difficulties of wealth for them was the sense of isolation. They felt different because they had money or they were concerned that people liked them just because of their wealth. Their children privately held the same fears and concerns, so it proved invaluable for the parents to share their stories of struggles and isolation. This normalized the feelings of the children and then they were able to problem-solve together.

Members of another family described the painful fallout of an event that they all thought should have been cause for celebration. The father had built a hugely successful business from the ground up, and he and his wife raised three happy and well-adjusted children. They were the "middle-class millionaires" who lived their lives below the radar. Then the father decided to take the business public. Suddenly it was a matter of public record that the family was worth two billion dollars. The family was completely unprepared for the emotional tsunami that hit them. They lost friends. They quickly gained new "friends" who were very interested in them and their newfound wealth.

I interviewed this couple a few years after this sudden money event, and they said the entire family had been struggling ever since. One of the parents and one of the children had had major bouts of depression, while one of the sons had essentially dropped out of life.

Any financial transition like this one will cause stress for individuals and the entire family. It doesn't matter whether the transition is a sudden decrease in wealth or a sudden increase. Both will disrupt the homeostasis of the family and create a ripple effect that typically involves stress, depression, addiction, fractured attention, and disharmony. The most important curative factor is for the individuals and family to talk openly about their feelings and normalize their behavior.

It's also crucial not to make any life-changing decisions for six months to a year because of the emotional churn of a financial transition. Susan Bradley, in her book *Sudden Money,* recommends what she calls a Decision Free Zone. She says anyone who has experienced a sudden money event is emotionally flooded and cognitively impaired for close to a year following the event. Therefore, they need to take a time out from any major decisions like buying a new home or giving money to friends or family.

Encourage Kids to Find Their Own Identity

A 67-year-old man from one of my client families told me, "It's my fundamental job as a dad to help my kids and grandkids develop their own sense of identity, because I know trying to be me is not going to work for them."

This man was typical of many of the wealth creators in families I see. It's common for men, or sometimes couples, to spend their lives working hard to build up a successful business. In their 60s, thinking about retirement, they really recognize that they missed out on a lot of the kids' lives when they were growing up. They wake up to the fact that it's time to shift the focus from helping the business succeed to helping the family succeed. This means becoming very intentional about the development of the kids and grandkids.

The elders in flourishing families make it a point to encourage younger family members to find their own paths and passions. They understand that it helps not only the individuals but also the family to be successful. In many cases, this is easier said than done. It's tough enough for any kids to develop their own identities, but in affluent families, when you have parents or grandparents that in many cases are larger than life, it can be even harder.

In one family, for example, a core value was education, and there was a tradition that everyone went to a particular Ivy League school. In fact, Grandpa had a building on the campus named after him. One granddaughter sent something of a shock wave through the family when she chose to go to a different university. The expectation that everyone would attend the family alma mater carried a lot of pressure, intentional or not.

This is one more reason that identifying core values is so important. It helps families separate the traditions that are important in passing on those values from those that are habits or expectations that can make it harder for family members to identify their own identities. In this family, the core value, education, had become enmeshed with an assumption, "we go to this university," which wasn't actually essential to the value.

Foster Leadership in Younger Generations

Brian, at 36, was the primary investment manager for his family's wealth and a managing partner in the family office. With a master's degree in financial planning and a decade of experience in investment banking, he was well qualified for the position.

Brian's grandfather had built a manufacturing business that allowed him to retire with wealth before he was 50, so the second and third generations in this family grew up in affluence. Brian described members of his own third generation as "dysfunctional" into their early adulthood. Of his two siblings and five cousins, all of whom had trust funds set up by their grandparents, he was the only one who had ever held a job. Fortunately, members of the family became alarmed at the pattern of idleness and began working with a financial coach and advisor. They clarified the family mission and vision, learned some ways to communicate more effectively, and began working together as a family to use their wealth in empowering ways.

One of the strengths that emerged for this family was a spirit of collaboration and flexibility. Brian's financial training and experience made him a logical choice to manage the family investments. Even more important, he became a leader in family discussions about the behavioral side of wealth. His leadership was accepted and encouraged, not only by his siblings and cousins, but by members of the older generations as well.

Fostering leadership, like other stewardship skills, is often done best by example. Most thriving families are headed by leaders rather than dictators. They understand the importance of emotional intelligence as well as business or financial skills, and they live a family value of humility.

One pattern I've seen quite often is that wealth creators spend their middle years as hard-driving entrepreneurs and business owners. That style tends to carry over into their parenting. Then in about their 60s, these same parents and grandparents move into more of a mentoring role in the family. Members of the second generation, on the other hand, are more likely to use the mentoring style from the beginning. One man summed it up this way: "My grandfather's style was, 'lead, follow, or get out of the way.' My father's approach was, 'gather information, collect ideas, and collaborate.'"

Author and family business consultant Dennis T. Jaffee, Ph.D., talks about the necessity for children to become "citizens of the family enterprise." Wealthy families that are successful in fostering well-prepared citizens intentionally invest in leadership for young adults, both as individuals and within the family. They encourage members of younger generations to develop their own mature voices. As younger family members move into leadership roles, those in the older generations are able to shift into advisory and mentoring positions as the respected and valued family elders.

Help Heirs Say Yes to Wealth

The job of parents to create optimal frustration for their children doesn't necessarily end when the kids grow up. One important place that it still applies is in legacy planning. The families I work with tend to be intentional about wanting to strike the right balance, where the wealth empowers their heirs and helps them build their own muscles instead of sapping their strength and energy. They want to support children financially in ways that feel right to both generations. Each family I work with finds that balance point a little differently. But rather than just passing on the wealth, they really are taking a look at how to pass it on with a spirit of stewardship rather than entitlement.

These are some of the strategies I've seen flourishing families use.

1. Maintain business values in the family. Something that surprised me, in talking with some of the families I interviewed for this book, is how many successful families treat their business like their family and their family like their business. The core values they talk about in the family, like integrity, honesty, and being respectful of each

other, are the same basic values that have made them successful as business people. In several cases, there were few boundaries between family and business. The core values of the business might be described in such terms as: be honest with your customers and employees, never look down on them, they work with us not for us, take pride in what you do, catch your employees doing something right. This would turn out to be the same way these business owners were parenting their kids.

2. Create a pattern of intentional choices and communication about participation in a family business. A few families I've worked with actively discourage younger generations from participating in the business owned by the wealth creator, wanting them to follow their own paths instead. Other families encourage kids and grandkids to be part of a family business, intentionally teaching them and preparing them for active roles. One crucial factor that's common in thriving families is to make clear distinctions between the roles, responsibilities, and rewards for family members who are owner/employees of the business versus those who are owners but not employees. Active training for family members who sit on boards of directors is also important. All these families emphasize that ownership of a family business is a responsibility, not an entitlement.

3. Establish an organized system of family governance. There are many ways to manage family assets and activities, some of which are described in more detail in Chapter Seven. What thriving families have in common is an organization that emphasizes communication and working toward common goals. Many families pay adult children to actively participate as members of a family board that oversees the management of investments and the use of shared assets. Sometimes that family board is

involved in giving as well, and sometimes families set up charitable foundations with their own separate boards.

4. Provide opportunities to learn from mistakes. Members of several families I interviewed talked about the value of making mistakes as long as the family culture encouraged owning up to, talking about, and learning from those mistakes. Some of them also pointed out the benefit for young adults of having some money of their own—preferably their own earnings—to make their own spending and investment mistakes with.

5. Encourage appropriate and healthy family connection. Members of flourishing families are interconnected but not rigid or enmeshed. As one family matriarch put it: "We try to give the kids a lot of encouragement and guidance without trying to control their lives. We always want to encourage them to stay close by, but still respect their privacy." This is a very difficult balancing act for most families. Families can live along a continuum where one end is *disengaged.* They have limited contact, value individualism over family identity, and convey a sense of "It's your life; make the best of it." At the opposite extreme is *enmeshment.* Here, parents are overly involved in their children's lives, individualism is discouraged, the children have a sense of needing to meet the needs of the parents, and the parenting is highly involved. These are what is frequently referred to as "helicopter parents." As parents, we need to find a balance point between the two extremes where we empower our children to lead their own lives while still knowing that our support is available when needed.

6. Teach kids how to talk about money. One third-generation young man told me, "Since one of the core values in this family is authenticity, it feels like a violation of that not to be open about how much money I have. But at

the same time, I don't want the money to set me apart from my friends. Plus, I don't want to be stupid and open myself up to being taken advantage of." One of the things we worked on with this man and his sisters was developing an "elevator speech" to reveal an appropriate amount about the family wealth without either minimizing or bragging about it.

7. Be open to learning. "Hire good advisors and be willing to learn what they have to teach you," is the way one wealth creator put it. In both his business and his personal life, this man never made the mistake of assuming that wealth and knowledge automatically went together. He listened to and learned from anyone he believed had something to teach him: his employees, his financial advisors, his peers, and, as they grew up, his children.

8. Give family members permission to enjoy the wealth. Wealth does not need to be seen as a burden or something to induce guilt. Members of flourishing families support each other in accepting the incredible gift of wealth and developing a sense of gratitude and appreciation. One family I've worked with says without apology that they "live large." One of their core values is to enjoy and appreciate the benefits that their wealth provides. They intentionally live out that value as part of managing the family money to empower the younger generations, just as much as they live the value of giving back to their communities. For them, living large means, "We don't need to apologize for being wealthy. We can enjoy it and also make a difference in our community and in our world."

9. Communicate about legacy plans. This is yet another reason for defining core values. Conflicts, unpleasant surprises, and manipulation are much less likely to be part of estate planning when everyone knows the family's core values and knows that legacy plans are consistent with

those values.

10. Foster a sense of stewardship. Fundamentally, thriving families see that they are the stewards of the wealth. They have a felt sense that they are to do good things with the wealth, care for it, increase it, and use it to create positive change. They understand that money is energy. Just like other forms of energy such as electricity, it can be destructive and harmful. Yet, if handled with care and grace, its energy can be beautiful and beneficial.

One of my goals in working with families is to help them think of inheriting family wealth in a different way. It is not a gift. It is not an entitlement. Instead, it is a transition. When the legacy planning is done in line with the family's values, when it is guided by strong communication, and when the heirs are prepared, that transition can be a smooth one.

CHAPTER SEVEN
EFFECTIVE FAMILY SYSTEMS

WHEN FAMILIES DEFINE their values and write clear mission statements, they are creating anchors or touchstones for the family—the *Why*. The family's vision for itself is the *What*. Those two elements of family success are essential to establish and clarify a family's identity.

There's one more component that is every bit as crucial in helping a family succeed. That is a system to effectively translate the family values and vision into action. This is the *How*. It includes the various aspects of managing the wealth and passing on the family legacy, such as financial planning, estate planning, trusts, and operating the family office. Another important but often overlooked piece of the How is family governance.

Governance, fundamentally, is the answer to the question, "How do we make decisions together as a family?" It provides ways to keep the vision and values at the forefront, foster good communication, and provide both accountability and support for family members. It is the structure and process used to implement the family values in relation to operating the family business, managing the family money, giving to causes that are important to the family, and leaving a legacy to future generations. The mission statement is the essential guide or anchor for the family in being successful. Ideally, everything they wish to accomplish becomes an extension of their core values. Governance is the process that makes that happen.

The need for a system to make decisions together as a family applies to families at all levels of wealth. The details of that system will vary from family to family. The governance needs of a family with $2 million in net worth will be different from those of a family with $20 million or $2 billion. The needs of a three-generation family with 10 or 11 members will differ from those of a family made up of dozens of members five generations removed from the wealth creators. I've worked with families that had complex 20-page documents to describe all the different approaches to governance, and with others that had a few paragraphs.

This chapter will describe a few approaches that different families use successfully, but each family needs to adapt these models and establish a structure that meets its unique needs. The ultimate guideline for the process is: "How can we best make decisions together, and how do we best support our values, mission, and vision?"

Designing a System of Governance

1. Start with What You Have

Every family has quirks, patterns, and tolerances that have developed over decades. Sometimes people are so busy being in the family that they don't have the time or the tools to work on the family system. The family may be generally happy, but still some members may see ways it could be stronger. It's not uncommon for family members to see the potential of others in the family but not recognize it in themselves. All of these factors affect the family's internal harmony. They need to be taken into account in designing a process for decision-making that will shape the family's collective impact outside of the family system and into future generations.

For families where no formal system of governance is in place, the best time to begin designing one is now. In a perfect world, families wouldn't wait until they were in crisis to set up a system to guide their decisions. Having the process in place makes it easier to deal with difficulties when they do show up. A system that fosters communication and shared values can address problems while they are still relatively minor and can even help prevent problems in the first place.

Of course, since we don't live in a perfect world, it may take a crisis to demonstrate how much a family needs some structure. When this is the case, the crisis can serve as the driving force to persuade family members to start making necessary changes. For example, in one family a very simple request turned into a significant learning experience. The children's nanny, who was well loved and had been with the family for a number of years, asked the mother in confidence if she could borrow several thousand dollars to attend to a personal matter. The mother, caught completely off guard, blurted out yes and wrote a check for $4,000. Then she began having second thoughts and feeling guilty. Her internal conversation went something like this: "Should I have given her money? Is it blurring boundaries? I have so much that it shouldn't be a big deal. Should I have consulted with my husband first?"

Fortunately, instead of keeping the incident a secret, she discussed it with others in the family. They realized that similar requests were likely to happen to various family members. It was agreed that they needed to have a policy to guide future decisions about making loans or gifts to friends and family members. The policy they developed included the following:

a. Anyone in the family would have a 48-hour cooling off

period prior to giving an answer.

b. The first-generation couple would have to consult with each other before giving an answer.

c. If the amount of the request was over $10,000, they would also consult with their financial advisor.

d. Members of the second generation, who were in their 30s, would follow the same process and would also consult with their parents.

The requirement to consult with their parents might seem like a restriction for the members of the second generation. What it actually did for them was remove a burden. When they were approached for money, they were able to say to friends or anyone else, "It really isn't my money but my parents' money, so I need run it by them and their advisors."

Having this structure was a huge relief for the family because they would no longer be caught flat-footed. It meant each family member wasn't personally approving or rejecting a request, but was following the family process for vetting requests.

2. Keep It Appropriately Simple

It's important to keep in mind that the system is designed to facilitate communication and decision-making, not become an end in itself. It needs to be detailed enough to be useful, but not so cumbersome that it is impractical and will sink under its own weight. The system is meant to support family members, not intimidate them. It also needs to be flexible enough so it can evolve as the family grows and its needs change.

One advantage of having a family governance system developed by most or all members of the family is that, when difficult decisions need to be made, the system itself can be the "enforcer." It can help separate financial decisions from family relationships and help family members understand, as one man put it, that "money isn't personal."

A useful resource that discusses keeping a system simple, especially for smaller families, is Patrick Lencioni's *The 3 Big Questions for a Frantic Family*. While the book focuses on defining values for a nuclear family, Lencioni's process can be a useful starting point for any family.

3. Focus on Strengths

In coming to an agreement about family governance, it's helpful to consider the family now versus 30 or 50 years from now. Often, when I'm working with a family in the midst of an important decision, I will ask them this question: "What decision would best support the stated purpose of the family, and what decision would best support your family 30 years from now?"

A long-term vision is vital to the success of a family for two important reasons. The first is that, just as in business—or in sailing, for that matter—you need to be clear about where you are going. That clarity generates the declaration, "This is where we are going as a family." It also moves the focus from, "What is best for me or my spouse?" to, "What is best for our family long-term?"

The second reason for a long-term vision is that wealth exacerbates a family's preexisting fault lines. The generational time clock can convert minor annoyances into brick walls of disunity. A strong system for guiding family decisions can help make the good better rather than allowing the rough spots to magnify.

My goal in working with families is always to help them build on their strengths, rather than emphasizing problems and weaknesses. This does not mean pretending problems don't exist or failing to address them. Focusing on what families already do well helps them become stronger and gives them more resources and options for solving the problems they do have. Because change occurs in the direction of our attention, concentrating on strengths helps families move from good to exceptional.

4. Foster Leadership within the Family

Thriving families understand the value of getting services, advice, and education from professional advisors. They commonly employ accountants, attorneys, financial planners, and other staff members to manage investments and run family offices. In their governance systems, they often bring in advisors and coaches to facilitate meetings and offer training to family members. They also understand the importance of sharing information to allow their advisors to work as a team.

At the same time, these families understand that providing expertise and facilitating communication are not the same as taking on leadership. Ideally, family members will develop long-term relationships of mutual trust and respect with their advisors. Yet in strong families, it remains clear to all parties that the family members are the ultimate decision-makers. They serve as an "executive board" to define the values, goals, and boundaries of the family. The advisors are the "executive staff" who manage the resources in accordance with those values and goals.

When families work with advisors over a long period of time, it's easy for both the professionals and members of the family to slip into a relationship where the "experts" take on more and more authority. In some cases, this can even become almost a parent/child dynamic with the advisors or employees in the parental role. They sometimes seem to feel more responsibility for the success of the family than the family members themselves do. This is a role reversal that, in the long term, doesn't serve anyone well.

As I tell families when I begin a coaching relationship with them, my long-term goal is always to work myself out of a job. In working with advisors, it's essential for everyone to keep in mind that the word "advisor" means exactly what it says. Members of successful families are wise enough to pay attention to the advice and expertise of the professionals they consult, but they are also wise enough to remember that the ultimate responsibility for decisions and leadership always rests within the family.

Developing that leadership and training leaders for the future is also a crucial aspect of long-term success for the family. For that reason, it's important for a family governance process to involve members of all adult generations.

5. Emphasize Ongoing Communication

Creating a family mission statement, as described in Chapter Three, lays the foundation for effective family governance. Building a workable system requires following up with regular communication, in part through regular family meetings. Most families I've worked with schedule these once or twice a year. It's common for these meetings to be facilitated by a coach or other support person and to include family financial advisors and other professionals as appropriate.

At these meetings, it's crucial to revisit the following questions each time: How are we doing living from our values? Are we successfully and reliably operating from this vision statement that we all worked so hard on crafting together? Many families begin each family meeting with a reading of their values and mission.

Many families build at least one meeting a year around a specific theme such as communication, preparing heirs, or giving. These meetings can also be used to work on concerns or emerging patterns that family members see as threats or potential threats. Once a particular issue is brought out, the family can address it, often with coaching or counseling from professional advisors. An important part of the process in many families is learning how to talk about money, especially the emotional and psychological aspects of wealth. It isn't enough just to decide it's important to communicate; people also need some training in how to communicate.

A practice I've seen in a number of thriving families is that, once an issue or theme comes up in a meeting, they follow up by spending additional time and resources on that issue. For example, if communication was the theme of a family meeting, during their interactions in the following months they would emphasize the key knowledge and practice the tools learned from that session. Or if tension or animosity between family members surfaced during a meeting, as can happen in any family, there was a commitment to work on that tension with the family coach or consultant.

This commitment to work to resolve conflicts is especially important in family businesses, where old patterns from childhood are often an impediment to the governance of the family.

This was the case with the Steiner family. They are kind, bright, good people, with a wonderful sense of humor. The father, Walter, is a fairly typical wealth creator who started from nothing, worked very hard, and has built a successful business. He and his wife have two sons who both chose to work in the family business. As Walter started thinking about his own retirement, he designated the oldest son, Jake, to be his successor as general manager. Yet Jake told me privately that he didn't want the responsibility and would rather stay on as the sales manager, a position he was well suited for and did well in. The younger son, David, was well qualified for the general manager position and was very interested in it.

The problem was that David and his father had a long history of conflict when it came to the business. The pattern was well known by the family and not at all difficult to unearth; the two men were just alike. Both were competitive, hard driving, controlling, and had a need to be right.

It took a handful of meetings with the three of us to sort out their differences. It helped a lot that both Walter and David were able to see the humor in how much alike they were. They realized that their pattern of annoyance with each other was harmful not only to them but also to the family. They also realized that, together, they were a powerful creative force.

Fundamentally, the families that are successful in the long term are willing to talk about their differences. They learn to not make each other wrong but to learn from each other and reliably operate from a shared purpose.

Many families make their meetings part of an annual family retreat. They regard it as a combination business meeting and family reunion or vacation, with time for fun being as important as the family meetings. The recreational times, of course, include the younger grandchildren and great-grandchildren as well as those old enough to participate in the more formal meetings. This helps establish the expectation for all generations that meeting regularly is a normal, important, and fun event that is part of what the family does.

Some common topics that I have helped families address at family meetings are:

Education and Family Development
- Communication
- Psychology of wealth
- Using tools such as Emergenetics Profiles to understand individual strengths and differences
- Creating an appreciative family culture
- Rebuilding trust
- Best practices of flourishing families
- Family purpose and vision
- Values retreat

- Impact of sudden wealth and wealth transitions
- Creating conversations about what wealth means
- Behavioral finance
- Philanthropy

Individual Development
- Personal and business coaching
- Leadership development
- Strategic life planning
- Living a life with purpose

6. Establish a Formal Structure

In addition to family meetings, most family governance systems include boards and committees that are responsible for decisions and overseeing specific areas. Some of those areas may be:

- Managing family wealth
- Managing shared assets such as vacation homes or airplanes
- Directing a "family bank" that makes loans or grants to family members
- Overseeing family foundations or other entities for charitable giving
- Educating and preparing heirs and future leaders

To be most effective, a family governance system will involve all generations of the family in appropriate ways. The following is one example of a way to think of roles and responsibilities in a four-generation family:

Generation One, Elders. This generation may be the wealth creators, often retired and in their 70s or 80s.

Their primary role is mentoring, advising, and resolving conflicts.

Generation Two, Seniors. Members of this generation may have the primary leadership and management roles in the family businesses. They also are active heads of the larger family enterprise—managing family wealth, shared assets or properties, and charitable foundations in ways that support the family's mission.

Generation Three, Young Adults. Members of this generation may also be actively involved in family businesses, or they may have separate careers. They are learning about the family enterprise and gradually moving into active participation. Another important role for this generation is to bring new energy and ideas into the family as they serve as a bridge to the future.

Generation Four, Children. The role of this generation is simply to be kids, growing up and learning the family legacy with the support and role modeling of all the previous generations.

Many families set up a specific process for making major decisions at family meetings. This may be a Family Council made up of all adult family members. Various committees and boards of directors, with representation from all adult generations, oversee aspects of the family enterprise like investments, charitable giving, and family activities and events.

Sample Family Governance Models

The following examples of governance models are based on systems that different families have used successfully.

Example A

This is a large family that now has descended seven generations from the original wealth. The members of Generation Five range in age from 40s to 60s, and members of Generation Six are moving into the family governance. One of this family's missions is to keep the family together, which is challenging because of its size. Their system of governance includes three organizational bodies. At the top is a Board of Directors. Family members are voted in by the family.

Below the Board of Directors are two equal entities: the Family Foundation Board and the Investment Company Board. The Family Foundation Board includes six family members voted into office by the family, along with outside board members selected by the family because of their expertise in philanthropy. The Investment Company Board is comprised of three family members voted in by the family and two outside members with diverse investment experience.

Example B

A family that I interviewed had an unusual structure in that they choose not to vote but to make all decisions through consensus. This has forced a culture of communication and staying with it. They insist on civility and inclusion, so anyone who goes over the line is quickly "busted." They honor differences, respect and defer to their elders, and emphasize that the wealth is a gift and with that gift comes responsibility. Yet they also value a sense of humor and lightness. Because of this model, the cousins are very close. In-laws and others who are not in the bloodline are not part of the family boards or included in the business meetings. They are invited to the family gathering/fun portions of the family meetings.

Example C

At the head of this family's governance system is a CEO of the family boards and partnerships. This family member is chosen by the family as the most qualified business person in the family. The CEO's job is to listen and learn from the family, seek alignment, and make decisions based on what is best for the family. The ultimate decision-making rests with the CEO, who will also be in close communication with the family office.

A Board of Advisors chosen by the family works with the CEO and helps with implementing policy. This is also a training ground for younger family members to learn more about the business and leadership.

A separate Investment Committee, chosen by the family and which may include members outside the family, also advises the CEO on investment decisions.

In addition, a Family Board, voted on by the family, addresses and supports the human capital of the family. Members of this board set up the family retreats and serve on subcommittees focused on education and family communication.

Example D

One family, with relatively few members even though it includes four generations, has as its ultimate decision-making body a Family Council made up of all family members (including in-laws) aged 21 and over. The Council meets annually and also schedules additional videoconferencing sessions as needed. A five-member Executive Board elected by the Family Council oversees day-to-day business and decisions.

Reporting to the Family Council and Executive Board are three committees, with members elected by the Family Council and representing each adult generation. The Investment

Committee, overseeing money management and investments, includes outside investment advisors as well as family members. The Family Foundation Board is responsible for charitable giving. The Education Committee organizes family retreats and meetings as part of its assignment to provide ongoing training to family members in areas such as communication, wealth management, and leadership.

Conclusion

We are all integral people. The many facets of our lives—our personalities, relationships, talents, knowledge, and wisdom—make us the unique individuals we are. Each of us to some extent is defined by the family system we are part of, and each of us in turn helps define that system. The underlying purpose of effective family governance is to help individuals rise to their own highest purpose with the support of the family system. At the same time, family members' individual accomplishments strengthen the family system. When individual and family achievement is fostered within the context of clear family values and a strong family mission, good families can become great families and accomplish great things in and for their communities.

CHAPTER EIGHT

COMMUNICATION AND CONNECTION

THE MITCHELLS, IN their 60s, still owned and managed a manufacturing company that had made them wealthy. One of the reasons they consulted me was their concern over their son. Allen had started his own company in a related industry, but he wasn't doing nearly as well as his parents had. In fact, he was mismanaging his business into near-bankruptcy.

When I started talking with Allen about ways to recover from his business crisis, he expressed a lot of frustration and finally said, "I hate this business." I asked the obvious question: "Then why are you in it?"

His answer was, "Mom and Dad expect me to be. It's the only way I can get their approval."

He was absolutely positive this was true. Yet when I went back to his parents, they told me, "We don't care what business he's in as long as he's happy. In fact, we'd just as soon he tried some other field that's less risky."

Once he understood that his parents didn't have the expectations he believed they had, Allen sold his company. He went back to college to get an advanced degree in the history that was his real passion, and he found his own niche as a professor at a community college.

Over the years I've seen many situations similar to this. Members of later generations in wealthy families, especially those with family-owned businesses, may build entire careers in jobs they don't like. Others may feel obligated to follow lifestyles they aren't comfortable with. In some families, unresolved conflicts can lead to tension and rifts that last for generations.

Many times, the roots of these long-term difficulties can be traced back to failed communication. The founder of a family business might assume, without ever saying so, that members of later generations will take over the business. Younger family members might assume, without ever asking, that they have to follow in the footsteps of their parents or grandparents. People make assumptions about what they think other people want, need, or expect. Yet no one ever knows whether those assumptions are accurate because the family doesn't talk about them. All these assumptions make for a family-wide guessing game that isn't any fun and that nobody wins.

Families that thrive, on the other hand, tend to communicate well. Of course, no family is going to have perfect communication, but the number-one factor in successful families is what I call skillful communication. This doesn't mean they talk about everything. By and large, though, they have a tendency to talk about the issues that need to be talked about. They do this in ways that don't put someone in a one-down position. They value openness and follow patterns of effective communication.

Skillful communication isn't going to look the same in every family. Different families have different comfort levels when it comes to closeness, spending time together, or involvement with family businesses or foundations. I've worked with families where parents and adult children live in the same area, talk almost daily, and get together often. I've also worked with families whose members are much more widely scattered and might connect with each other only a few times a year. Either style can work well for a given family.

Communication and connection are not the same as enmeshment or dependency. Consider a scale from 1 to 100 where

1 means "enmeshed" and 100 means "disengaged." In an enmeshed family, parents are overly involved in their adult children's day-to-day affairs. "The family" is a specter looming over individual families that keeps them from living their own lives. There are few boundaries and little respect for privacy or individuality. The children have a difficult time emancipating and forming an identity separate from their parents.

Members of a disengaged family, on the other hand, have little contact, know little about one another's daily lives, may care little about each other, and have little or no sense of family identity. The boundaries in these families are rigid, and the children are left with a feeling of disconnection and lack of care. To make matters even more confusing for children, some families have each parent at opposite extremes. One example is an enmeshed mother and a disengaged father. These extremes set up an internalized parent for children, where they in essence learn to parent themselves in a similar way as they mature. Enmeshed children will often appear nervous and insecure, where disengaged children may grow up disconnected from their feelings and relationships in general.

Neither extreme is conducive to family and individual success. Yet a fairly broad range in the middle of the scale represents different styles and comfort levels that can allow families to flourish. Families all across that range can interact in ways that foster effective communication.

Unfortunately, communication is another of those areas that most of us believe to be important, but that most of us don't know how to do well. I referred earlier to a 2005 study by the Allianz Group that showed three-fourths of affluent Americans believe talking with children about money is important, but that only a third has actually had those conversations.

What I've found in working with families is this typical lack of communication isn't because we're lazy, or we're neglectful, or we don't care. It's because most of us don't know how or where to start. The parents often don't want children and grandchildren to live with ambiguity about expectations, yet they don't know how to provide clarity. There is sometimes a bit of collusion with younger family members, too. Members of the second generation can see that Mom and Dad are tense about certain subjects, and they don't want to be disruptive or cause more tension so they don't ask about those subjects.

Few of us have ever had any training in communication. Learning to be skillful communicators is the real challenge for families. It is also the real opportunity. Almost all families, given the chance to learn some tools and skills, can become effective communicators. Family members can get past the awkwardness and difficulty that stand in the way of talking about important issues. It is possible to have productive, respectful conversations about subjects like who is expected to be part of the family business or how to provide fairly for later generations. Having worked with many different families over the years, I have learned that what matters most is not trying to find "perfect" solutions. Instead, the real power lies in having conversations. After all, we can change patterns in families, one conversation at a time.

Speech Acts and Clarity in Communication

For me, parenthood has often been an interesting blend of appreciation and hard-earned lessons, many of them provided by my oldest daughter. As she entered her teen years, one of the most obvious changes was her style of communication. All of a sudden, the rules that I was clear about seemed to lack clarity on her part. For example, in my mind the issue of what time to be home had been established. She had to ask permission to go out, and when she did her curfew was 10:00 on school nights and midnight on weekends. In addition, she always was supposed to let me know when she came home. Yet if she got home 20 or 30 minutes late and I confronted her, the response was, "You didn't tell me to be home by 10:00." I quickly learned that clarity around requests and promises became paramount. If my communication lacked precision, she had an uncanny ability to capitalize on any ambiguity.

This ability to find loopholes in communication certainly isn't limited to teenagers. One of my friends told me this story about her youngest son at about age five. He often woke up early on weekends, and he would knock on his sister's bedroom door to wake her up so he would have someone to play with. His parents told him specifically that he wasn't allowed to knock on her door. The next Saturday morning, they heard him making rapping sounds outside his sister's room. He wasn't breaking the rules by knocking on the door. But no one had said anything about the floor, so he was industriously thumping on the carpet.

Whether we're dealing with teenagers, small children, or other adults, clarity is one of the essentials of good communication. We tend to think of communication as being passive. Yet in reality it is active. It causes things to happen, intended and unintended. The more conscious we become about communicating, the more effectively we will transmit the messages we actually intend to send.

One way to move from hoping our communication is effective to making it active is to understand the different types of "speech acts." The following categories are based on the work of Fernando Flores, a business consultant, former member of the Chilean government, and co-author of several books. He describes the following set of speech acts: Assertions, Assessments, Declarations, Requests, Offers, and Promises.

Assertions vs. Assessments. Suppose I make two statements: I am a man and I am tall. What is the difference between the two? "I am a man" is a fact. It is an *assertion* that can be measured and proven. "I am tall" is subjective, an *assessment* that is an opinion or judgment. (Of course, in some specific circumstances, a statement such as, "I am the tallest person in this group," could be a measurable fact.)

Problems arise when we allow assessments to live as assertions. It may not cause much difficulty in my life if I assume "I am tall" to be a fact. It's a different matter, though, if I live with an assertion such as "I am stupid" and believe it to be an unexamined fact. I will conduct my life as if that statement is true, when it is really an assessment. The result will be damaging to my sense of self-worth, my relationships, and my career. Similar damage is caused by the assessments we make about other people that we treat as assertions.

In working with families, I often hear statements like, "I'm not good with money." It's important to find out what that assessment is based on. Where did it come from? Some of us spend the majority of our lives trapped inside of and living according to false assessments. I've seen this countless times: Person A forms an assessment of Person B, the assessment is frozen as a fact, Person A has long forgotten that the assertion was a story made up based on an assessment, and Person A makes decisions about Person B based on the initial assessment. The initial assessment may have been completely inaccurate. Even if it contained some truth back when it was made, it may well be false years later. It's common to see siblings, for example, basing their adult relationships on assessments made on both sides when they were children. The relationship between two people today is still being shaped by data that is long out of date.

What is the speed of an opinion? Fast. If we want to have stronger relationships based on effective communication, it's important that we don't allow our opinions of ourselves and each other to live as facts.

Declarations. These are the most active of all of the speech acts. A declaration creates new possibilities and new actions. It gets your attention. Mathew Budd, author of *You are What You*

Say, says: "A declaration is an utterance in which someone with the authority to do so brings something into being that wasn't there before." A good example of a declaration was President Kennedy's statement in 1961 that "America will put a man on the moon within this decade." Having the authority to make the declaration, he provided a context for action.

Family mission statements like the ones described in Chapter Three are declarations. They provide leadership and guidance. When family members live up to those declarations, they build mutual trust and communicate that they take the values and mission of the family seriously.

Requests and Offers. These speech acts are crucial in negotiating, planning for the future, and helping family members work together. In thriving families, people are able to have conversations with family members and coordinate future actions. They are able to make realistic commitments and keep them. They can ask for help as appropriate. They can accept help and also accept that sometimes the answer to a request for help is "no."

Many of us have learned to make requests indirectly by hinting or manipulating. We may dilute our requests to reduce the chance of the other person saying no. Sometimes we make hidden "contracts" that we don't communicate to the other person and often aren't even consciously aware of ourselves. An example of this might be, "If I go to the symphony with you on Saturday night, you'll leave me alone to play golf on Sunday." On a larger scale, these hidden contracts might involve assumptions such as, "We'll pay for the kids' college educations, and in return they'll choose careers that support the family business." This kind of indirect communication is a setup for misunderstanding, resentment, and frustration for all parties.

Well-communicated requests are specific, respectful, and direct. In many cases, they also have clear deadlines. An example is, "Before wrapping up this meeting I want to check to make sure we are aligned on expectations. You agreed to have the final draft of the report to me by 5:00 p.m. Thursday so I can present our findings to the board by noon Friday."

A request like this gives the other person the opportunity to respond in one of four ways:

1. Saying yes. "Sure, I'll have it done by then."
2. Saying no. "I didn't say I would have the final version done, just that I would make the changes we talked about and have a second draft for you to look at. I can't do the final draft till I get feedback from the rest of the committee members."
3. Asking for time to respond. "I'm not sure I'll be able to get all the information I need in order to get it done on Thursday. Let me check and I'll call you in the morning."
4. Making a counter-offer. "I have appointments all day tomorrow and Thursday. If I have my assistant put in the changes we discussed today and get that to you in the morning, could you make the revisions to finish the report? Then I could be available on Friday if the board members have any questions."

Promises. Families that communicate well create an environment of personal responsibility. In order for families to thrive, members need to be able to count on people to say what they will do and do what they say. A promise is a commitment to do or not do something. When we make authentic promises, we assume responsibility and move from good intentions to actions. A promise is a way of saying, "You can count on me."

One of the difficulties with promises is our reluctance to say no, even when we know we probably aren't going to be able to live up to a commitment. Yet it is more respectful of others to say no in the first place than to say yes and then let them down by breaking the agreement. Not making promises lightly, but living up to the promises we do make, is a powerful way to build trust.

Expectations

Just as in the story of the Mitchell family at the beginning of this chapter, expectations are the most significant cause of breakdowns in communication. When we don't know what another person wants from us, it makes us crazy. Yet the ironic part is that, even though we hate it when we have to guess what someone else wants or needs, most of us still find it very hard to clearly state our own expectations of others.

This isn't because we're deliberately being difficult. Much of the time, it's because we assume the other person already knows what we know, wants what we want, or values what we value. In part, this is because each of us has a set of unconscious beliefs and assumptions, based on our own personalities and life experiences, about how the world works. Those beliefs are so automatic, and so obvious to us, that we assume any sane, rational person with any common sense whatsoever must share them. Therefore, we don't realize there's any need to state our expectations. Applying this to the earlier example of my daughter and her weeknight curfew, I might be making a couple of assumptions. One would be that she believes the 10:00 curfew we agreed to several months ago is reasonable and is still in force. Another might be that she would naturally want to get to bed early on a school night.

Another reason we aren't clear about our expectations is that we don't want to be rude or unkind. We don't want to attack people, appear to question their judgment, or treat them as if they are incompetent. Again, I might see reminding my daughter to be home by 10:00 as nagging her or treating her like an irresponsible child.

Finally, of course, we want to avoid conflict. Most of us haven't been taught communication skills, especially within our families. We aren't likely to see differences of opinion or conflicting needs as opportunities to negotiate. Instead, we tend to take them personally and end up in arguments. By not stating our expectations directly, we hope we can avoid disagreements. What often happens, of course, is that the disagreements are simply postponed. If I don't specifically tell my daughter to be home by 10:00, we won't have any argument about her curfew before she leaves. Instead, we might have a very uncomfortable talk when she comes in at 10:30.

The need in wealthy families for older generations to be clear about their expectations for children and grandchildren raises another issue. Just because expectations are explicitly stated doesn't necessarily mean they are reasonable or appropriate for others. A common example is the assumption that kids or grandkids will take over or be involved in a family business. There's nothing inherently bad or wrong about expectations like these. Often, they aren't about being unwilling to support the younger family members' independence. Instead, they are usually based on assumptions that the kids are just like their parents and want the same things the parents want.

Addressing conflicts like these goes back to Flores's concept of requests and offers. Once an expectation is expressed, a request or offer has been made. This opens the door to talk about it. The person receiving the request has the opportunity—as well as the responsibility—to accept it, reject it, or negotiate. Again, what matters most in these situations is not which answer is the best or right one. What is most important to support and strengthen the family is to have the conversations.

Another important factor when it comes to expectations is learning to be realistic about the ones we have for others. For example, suppose a brother and sister have a long-time pattern of failed commitments and broken promises. A typical occurrence would be their agreeing to share the cost of an expensive gift for their parents' anniversary. She buys it, but he never gets around to paying his share. A series of incidents like this eventually should make it clear to her that she can't expect him to keep his promises. Continuing to make agreements with him will just set her up for more disappointment and resentment. Instead, she can reduce her own stress by choosing not to enter into agreements that he is unlikely to keep.

In situations like this, it's wise to set limits on how much we expect from or trust the other person. Continuing to expect something that another person can't or won't provide will just damage the relationship further. Managing our own expectations doesn't mean we end the relationship or stop loving the other person. It just means we choose not to continue participating in a pattern of behavior that isn't good for either of us. Sometimes, setting limits in one area of a relationship allows us to move forward in other ways and can actually be a first step toward making the relationship stronger.

Communication and the Brain

Recent research in neuroscience has given us some useful insights into how the brain affects our interactions with other people. This is extremely useful information to know, in part because it helps us better understand ourselves. I also find it helps families to see themselves less judgmentally. All of us find ourselves in situations where something or someone "pushes our buttons" and triggers emotional responses that may seem irrational. Many times, we see these responses as dysfunctional or abnormal. Actually, they are about as normal as human beings get. Knowing how the human brain creates those emotional reactions can help us understand and get past them so they no longer block our communication.

The human brain has evolved this way: above the brain stem we have the more primitive amygdala, which some people call the lizard brain or reptilian brain. Then the mid-brain evolved, followed by the cortex and the prefrontal cortex. When we're reading, thinking, or learning facts we're primarily using the prefrontal cortex. We go through much of our adult lives with the prefrontal cortex engaged.

But from an evolutionary perspective, the amygdala has been around a lot longer than the prefrontal cortex. We can't bypass it. It is always on, scanning the environment for differences or possible threats. It's like an early warning detector or alarm. If it sees a threat of any kind, the bell goes off. It signals us to respond with one of four basic behaviors. We're going to fight, flee, freeze, or appease.

The amygdala's a good thing to have, even essential. Thank goodness our ancestors had it or they would never have survived and none of us would be here. The problem in today's world, though, is that the amygdala cannot discern the difference between a physical threat and a social threat. When we are involved in a family meeting, arguing with a spouse, or negotiating through a conflict with a teenager, the amygdala may react to what it perceives as threats. It cues one of the four protective responses even in situations where those responses aren't helpful.

Generally, each person develops what I call a signature style. When our buttons are pushed in some way, we'll probably default to one or perhaps two of the responses. We don't consciously choose these styles; they grow out of both our personalities and our early experiences. A fight response usually means we'll get angry and argumentative. Fleeing can be physically leaving a situation or can also take the form of emotionally withdrawing. Freezing is just what it sounds like—not responding either physically or verbally. When we appease, we'll try to smooth over a disagreement, offer a compromise, or even give in completely to whatever the other person seems to want.

Suppose, as an example, when a man's alarm is triggered his first reaction is to appease. He may only be in that mode for a few minutes, and then typically his next move is to fight. Since

God has a perfect sense of humor, chances are his wife is just the opposite. She might tend to fight and appease, or fight and flee. This can make an argument pretty interesting.

These different signature styles can create a great deal of frustration when we try to communicate, especially around issues where we have a lot of tension and conflict. Learning to identify our default responses, as well as those of our family members, can give us some useful insights into why our discussions and arguments follow the patterns they do. In one business I worked with, for example, four cousins operated a family company. We found that three of them had fight/flee signature styles and the fourth had appease/flee. Knowing this helped them understand why they had so much trouble making decisions.

Knowing one another's signature styles can also help reduce the emotional triggering that can happen during an argument or tense situation. Suppose a husband's first default response is to fight, while his wife's is to freeze. If they know this about each other, then when a conflict comes up, she may be able to think, "Okay, he's going to come off as angry because his default signature style is fight first. But that doesn't necessarily have anything to do with me." For his part, he may be able to remember, "If she doesn't say anything, that doesn't mean she's mad. I just need to give her more time to respond."

It also can be helpful to learn some techniques to help avoid the emotional reactions triggered by the amygdala so we can have cortex-to-cortex conversations. Suppose I go to a person I'm having a conflict with, and the first thing that comes out of my mouth is one of the following:

- "Why did you do that?"
- "What were you thinking?"
- "I can't believe you did that!"
- "You were wrong."
- "Why are you being such a jerk?"

The other person's amygdala is immediately going to respond with an emotional, defensive answer, and before we know it we're shouting at each other. Instead of doing anything to solve the original problem, we're piling new conflict on top of what was already there.

Suppose, instead, I try a statement like one of these:

- "This is what I think is happening, but I may not be seeing it right."
- "Can you help me understand … ?"
- "What more can you tell me about … ?"
- "What do you need me to understand about … ?"

These don't push the other person's buttons and generate that emotional, defensive response. Asking for more information rather than attacking the other person helps keep the discussion at the cortex level. When we ask questions that need to be answered by the cortex rather than making attacks that trigger the amygdala's protective reaction, we are more able to keep the conversation focused on solving the problem at hand.

Another important aspect of the brain that is helpful to know is what I call its negativity bias. Why is it that we pay so much more attention to criticism than we do to compliments? I used to be a college professor, and I would get student evaluations at the end of each semester. Suppose 30 or 40 students loved my class and rated it as the best one they'd ever had—and one person said it was awful and a total waste of time. Of course, the one negative evaluation is the one I would lose sleep over and remember the longest.

This negativity bias comes from the amygdala. It is intended to be protective. The amygdala's job is to remind us to pay attention to the early warning signs, to the negative thing, because it could come after us or even kill us. This is why, as individuals and as families, we tend to focus on what's wrong versus what's right. Once we know that negativity bias is just basic human behavior, we can start learning to focus on the positives instead. There's an old adage that "change occurs in the direction of our attention." If we're focusing on what's wrong, we'll get more of what's wrong. When we focus on what's right in the family, we can really steer the conversation to something that's a lot more useful and productive.

Trust

Trust is at the heart of all communication. Knowing we can believe what other family members say, that people will keep their promises, and that they won't gossip or manipulate is foundational to effective communication.

One question I usually ask in sessions with families is, "What qualities and behaviors create trust?" Some of the common answers are: consistency, loyalty, honesty, truth-telling, not gossiping, integrity, protecting confidences, and unconditional love.

In some families trust has been severely damaged, and an essential task is restoring it. What qualities restore trust? The answers I hear to this question include all the same qualities that create trust in the first place. In addition, people typically list the following: empathy, communication, forgiveness, insight/understanding, openness, accountability, humility, and love.

Because we all are human and we all make mistakes, we have many different ways of damaging trust among those we care about. Over the years I've heard a great many stories. While the details may vary, what I've learned is that there are three primary reasons for breakdowns in trust: Character, Communication, and Capability.

Character damages trust when people act without integrity. It is involved with behavior such as lying, breaking promises, gossiping, and cheating.

Communication (or more precisely, miscommunication) usually comes down to a matter of unspoken expectations or misunderstanding on both sides.

Capability becomes a factor when people are expected to do or commit to do something that is beyond their ability. The expectation may come from someone else or from themselves. They can't live up to the expectation, so the trust is damaged.

What's interesting about these three factors is the way we see them in ourselves and others. I'll ask people to think about a time their trust was violated by someone else, and then to judge which of the three reasons was behind it. The majority say "Character." Then I ask them to think about a time they violated someone else's trust and what the reason was. They almost always say, "Miscommunication."

Certainly, there are times when character is the cause of a breakdown in trust. In many cases, though, a neutral party who hears both sides of a story would see that miscommunication is a major factor. It's helpful when we can develop the habit of giving others the same benefit of the doubt and credit for good intentions that we give ourselves. When we start out by assuming a violation of trust is due to miscommunication rather than lack of character or competence, we are more likely to be able to work together to rebuild trust.

At the same time, it's not helpful to be so naïve that we ignore issues of character. All family members have to be accountable for who they are and what they do. Otherwise, it holds back the progress of the rest of the family. This is one more reason why building a family culture of integrity is so important.

Communication Tools

In working with families, I encourage them to use a variety of approaches to build stronger communication skills. These are a few that I have found most helpful.

Listening

Most of us, I believe, tend not to listen well. It isn't a skill that we're usually taught, so developing it is essential. It's especially important in wealthy families to listen to one another around issues of vulnerability about the money. The more comfortable people are internally with themselves and the money, the easier it is to respond to questions or challenges from outside the family about the wealth.

The families that I interviewed and have worked with are typical of most families in that they don't talk directly about money. It is an uncomfortable topic. Because the issue is largely hidden, misinformation abounds. One common pattern in affluent families is that Mom or Granddad was really smart and made a lot of money building a business. Once successful, they didn't necessarily share details of the hardship, the struggles, and the failures they encountered along the way. Their children and grandchildren, then, are left thinking it should be easy and that their own struggles are unique. Another assumption among family members is that, in order to be accepted, they have to go into the family business or have a personality like a particular parent. Sometimes they find out years later that the happiest kids are the ones who found their own paths.

This is another of the reasons that the Values Retreat and early Family Meetings are so important. It may be the first time that the parents have spoken very directly about their wishes for the family and the money, what values they hope to see in the family, and the desired vision that they have for the family. It is also a place where the family can openly discuss the burden of wealth and their fears or insecurities. Some families reported that the most valuable aspect of family meetings was taking the time to truly listen to one another.

Families need to have conversations whenever there's a new money event. Some examples of significant events would be inheritances, selling a business, experiencing serious financial losses, or taking a business public so that the family's net worth becomes public information.

In addition, I recommend holding regular family meetings. One of the benefits of these sessions is the opportunity they provide to practice listening. In facilitating family meetings, one of the most important aspects of my job is to hold the space for conversations. My role is not to tell family members what they should do, but to facilitate the discussions that help them make the decisions that are best for them. Sometimes, as part of this process, I ask family members who are getting together for a particular purpose to come up with guidelines for the discussion at that meeting. They usually come up with rules such as not interrupting, protecting confidences, and allowing everyone an opportunity to speak. The guidelines work because the members of the group own them, and they also work because they encourage people to listen.

A lot has been written on the topic of communication, and I have been influenced by a number of people, but I have learned more than I may ever appreciate from a dear friend and colleague, Mickey Connolly. He and Richard Rianoshek wrote a book called *The Communication Catalyst,* which I highly recommend. Some of the ideas and tools that I refer to in this chapter are influenced by or taken directly from that book.

One of the tools that I have altered slightly is the Ladder of Listening.

Bio reactive listening is related to the emotional response that comes from our amygdala. This is when we are "listening" through an emotional filter that has us judge the opinion of the other person. This is usually through the harsh light of negative opinion that has us critique and criticize the other person. In this type of listening we get zero points because nothing of any value is occurring, other than us expressing directly or indirectly our point of view.

Ladder of Listening

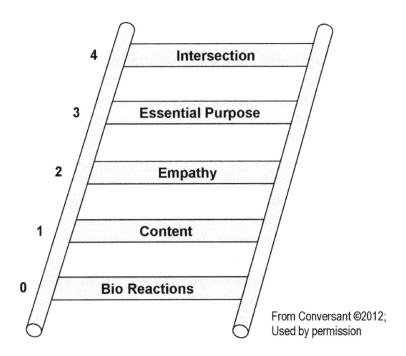

From Conversant ©2012; Used by permission

We get one point for *content*, that is, "Do I understand the details of what you are saying?" This is the beginning phase of mirroring, where I can repeat back what you are saying and I am beginning to take it in.

As mirroring evolves, we begin to understand the feelings that are related to the content. Often in life when we are arguing, whether it is about money or whose turn it is to take out the garbage, there are underlying feelings that are not being addressed.

We get two points for *empathy*, understanding what it feels like for the other person. While this is an important step and is where most communication models stop, I suggest that there are two more steps up the ladder.

Getting at *essential purpose* is when we come to truly understand why this issue is so important to the other person. It is what is at the core or the heart of an issue. I remember a few years ago I worked with a couple who were arguing about buying a second vacation home. The wife was saying she wanted one and the husband was saying it would be an impractical purchase. They already had an oceanfront vacation home. The husband also came armed with a set of facts from their financial advisor showing that, because of the real estate market, this was really not a good time to buy another vacation home. This argument had been simmering between this couple for months, and most of their time had been spent in bio reactive listening.

I asked the wife to explain why this was important to her, and I asked the husband to temporarily put his point of view on the shelf and to use the ladder of listening to get at the heart of the matter. Initially she talked about the general vision she had of a cabin in the mountains and how much fun it would be. As he began to truly listen, he asked her more about her feelings and why it was so important to her. As she continued talking, what began to emerge was her essential purpose for the new vacation home: to serve to unite the family. Two of their children had been estranged from the family, and seldom did they all get together. As their oldest son put it, the beach house was "the scene of the crime." It held some bad memories.

As the wife tearfully described her dream of this mountain cabin as a neutral place where kids and grandkids could gather to create new memories, the couple found a shared *intersection* where they could both stand. Creating a new beginning for the family was important to both of them, and a second vacation home could be the vehicle to achieve that shared purpose. The husband was also relieved to learn that the picture he had in mind, of an expensive home next to a ski slope, was not what his wife wanted or what was needed to support their purpose. The couple agreed to sell the beachfront home and to include their children in the search for a new home in the mountains.

Many times the primary barrier to listening is that we already think we know what the other person thinks or feels. Real listening is being fully present and listening not only to the point of view of the other person, but to their concerns and what is truly important to them.

Privacy vs. Secrecy

There is an old saying in Alcoholics Anonymous that "we are only as sick as the secrets we keep." That saying is trying to get at the destabilizing effect of powerful secrets like "someone in the family is addicted or has a mental illness and we are not to talk about it." Not talking about something that is already felt and experienced is an emotional pattern for the entire family that fosters confusion, conflict, and shame.

On the other hand, every family has secrets that are harmless, appropriate, and that even support the health and well-being of the family. One easy example would be a family conspiracy to hide a surprise gift or celebration. There are also certain issues between a husband and wife that are not a child's business.

The challenge for families is to distinguish between innocuous secrets and those that can harm a family if they are not acknowledged. Not talking about wealth can be one of those harmful secrets. In one of my interviews for this book I spoke to a man who was a self-made millionaire many times over. He spoke passionately about both his career and his family. He and his wife had four children in high school and college. When I asked him about financial and emotional preparation for his kids around the wealth, he said he hadn't spoken to them yet. He expressed genuine concern that if they knew how much he was worth it might spoil them or ruin their lives. I suggested that, in this day of online information and social media, it was reasonable to assume that his children already had a good idea how much he was worth. It was far more likely that they had a lot of unanswered questions about what it meant for them and the family. No matter how well-intentioned our motives are for keeping secrets about money, avoiding the subject can create a lot of made-up stories and conflicted feelings. Even when the conversations are difficult, it is far better to address those concerns directly.

While it is important to talk openly about money within the family, it is equally important to set boundaries about what is shared outside the family. There are two kinds of boundaries, internal and external. Internal boundaries refer to your sense of self and the confidence that you have in trusting your feelings. Emotional maturity and having healthy internal boundaries means knowing that just because you have a feeling doesn't mean you need to express it. It is having a level of discernment.

External boundaries involve setting limits with other people around what you will do or won't do. It is being respectful of others and respectful of yourself. It is honoring your feelings and not giving yourself away or allowing others to run over you.

Many families struggle with setting appropriate boundaries about what to say about their wealth. The bottom line is that it is no one else's businesses. Yet wealth is visible, and it isn't helpful or healthy for family members to pretend it doesn't exist or to be secretive about it.

A number of the families I work with are private about their wealth. One family, for example, had done an amazing job of intentionally staying below the radar. They even had a value to be humble with their wealth, and they frowned on public displays of wealth. This was a consistent value for each member of the family. Then, for a variety of reasons, they decided they wanted to form a family foundation to increase their level of philanthropic giving and contribution in their community. This made their wealth more visible. They had to come to terms with what to say about the money and how to say it.

What I often help families do is not only decide how much information they want to share publicly, but also to practice what to say in various circumstances. One tool we use is to help each family member craft an "elevator speech" they can use. They can rehearse how to respond if someone they barely know asks about the wealth, what to say if a friend or colleague inquires, or what to say if a close friend asks.

We also help them practice what to do or say if a friend asks for money. A number of families find it helpful to set up a system to refer all such requests to a third party. They teach family members to respond with something like this: "I'm not in a position to respond to any requests for money. If it's a foundation question, please contact the administrator of the foundation." Or if it is a request for a loan, "The family policy is to funnel all of those requests to our financial advisor."

No matter what level of privacy a family feels comfortable with, it's important to think through the questions that people may ask and to set up boundaries around those questions. One thing any wealthy family can count on is that people will ask questions. The more prepared family members are to answer them, the better.

Maintaining Files

All of us as family members have internal "files" on one another. These contain the perceptions and expectations we have about each person. The information in the files is both positive and negative, and all of it is based on a limited perspective. In families, many times these files are outdated. They are full of assessments about ourselves and other family members that we hold as facts. These assessments may go back to early childhood: "Paige always gets her way because she's the youngest," or "Colin is bossy and controlling."

Our brains try to ascribe meaning to everything around us and are always trying to make sense of things. This is why we come up with stories, based on our previous impressions as well as the current situation, to explain what's going on. Those stories make up a "file." Then we selectively reinforce the file over the years, supporting the stories with other evidence. This is confirmation bias, which means our brains are subconsciously always looking for evidence to support our perceptions. Any information that contradicts our assessments tends not to get filed. In addition, our minds focus on or even make up stories that confirm our biases. In time, the stories stop being stories and we assume them to be facts.

We have a lifetime of stories about who others in the family are. The files are so constricted and stuffed with old information that they don't allow us to breathe. Some of that material never was true. Other old information was based on the truth once upon a time, such as "That's the way my sister was when we were in elementary school." It may no longer be valid years later, but we don't question that story. For one thing, our brains are lazy, and it's easier to hang on to pre-existing prejudices than to change them with new information. Besides, we don't necessarily want to change our impressions. If my sister has always been the "bad kid" in my mind, that means I am the "good kid." Updating the story might mean adjusting my perception of myself as well as my perception of her.

The process of maintaining these files is crucial to rebuilding trust. I call the process "maintaining" rather than "updating," because ongoing attention to the files is so essential. Our brains tend to default back to what they know and what is familiar, so it's important to keep refreshing our perceptions by paying attention to the new information. This awareness is important so we don't keep creating new erroneous files. As parents especially, it's helpful to catch our own stories about our kids while they're still fresh, before they harden into perceived "facts" and become more difficult to change.

I often ask family members to do the following exercise. It can be done through one-on-one conversations if people are comfortable with that approach. For families who are just beginning to build their communication skills, it may be more helpful to write out the exercises individually and have the option of sharing them or not.

a. Write down a situation with someone in this family that you would like to improve. What story do you have in your file on this person that undermines your success in working together, communicating, or feeling comfortable together? It's often a good idea to start with a smaller issue rather than a significant one.

b. Decide in your own mind whether you're open to amending this file.

c. If you are willing to amend the file, come up with a game plan for doing so. Write down what you will do and set a time limit for doing it. If you're comfortable, tell the other person your plan.

d. This is the hard part. Carry out your plan.

There are three ways that a process like this helps us to change our perceptions of each other and our behavior toward each other.

1. Internal shifts that the other person perceives. It's amazing how much change can happen at a quantum or intuitive level, even if nothing is said out loud. All of us, in

133

varying ways, perceive what other people feel about us. So if one person changes his or her internal story about another. that can change the relationship even if the two of them don't talk about it. Even if the only change is my being open to the possibility that my stories may not be true, that can create a huge shift.

2. Listen to and learn from each other. Having conversations about our perceptions of each other, without attacking or judging, can be powerful ways to learn whether our assessments are true. Beginning these conversations takes one person approaching another with a non-confrontational statement such as: "I think this is what's going on, but I may be wrong. Can you help me understand … ?" All of us want to be heard, and many times all it takes to get someone to tell his or her side of a story is simply asking, with genuine interest and concern.

3. Take responsibility. If your file on another person has created harm, changing the file may include taking responsibility for your part in that harm and making amends. Most of the time, there is responsibility on both sides, so blaming yourself for the whole misunderstanding is most likely just another inaccuracy in the file. Making amends often includes three actions: offering a sincere apology, doing what you can to make things right, and making a commitment not to repeat the harm in the future. In some cases, making amends could cause more harm than good. In that case, see number one above: your changed perceptions and behavior usually will still improve the relationship.

The process of maintaining files starts with self-insight and understanding. It's also important to be aware of the files we keep on ourselves and to take responsibility for and be willing to change those perceptions as well. Some of the stories that create the most damage are the ones we tell ourselves about ourselves. A common one I see in wealthy families is, "I'm not as good as Mom or Dad," especially for the kids and grandkids of powerful, successful wealth creators who are seen as larger than life. Again, just becoming open to the possibility that what we believe about ourselves is really a made-up story can be a significant shift.

Appreciating and Building on the Family's Strengths

When I begin working with a family that is having trouble communicating, one of the first things I ask them is to tell me about some of their successes as a family. What times can they remember when they worked well together? What achievements are they proud of? What do they appreciate and respect about themselves as a family?

We then begin to pull all of the answers together to remind them of their core values. Almost always, this is the beginning of a transformation. Helping family members focus on their strengths lifts their spirits and helps them reconnect emotionally with each other and with the values that define them as a family. The more deeply they connect, the more openly and effectively they are able to communicate. This strength-based approach emphasizes moving forward by not focusing on problems, but by building on existing strengths. It keeps the family members' attention on what is possible.

Of all of the issues that I address in my work with families, communication is the most crucial. Miscommunication is the number-one reason for breakdowns in families, so it is vital that skillful communication is emphasized again and again.

CHAPTER NINE
REBUILDING A DAMAGED FAMILY CULTURE

THIS IS THE chapter where we talk about that enormous elephant in the living room. The one called "drugs, alcohol, and dysfunction."

One of the popular misperceptions about wealth, particularly inherited wealth, is that it creates a culture of addiction and other self-destructive behavior. This perception is supported by all the attention paid to celebrities whose legal difficulties, relationship difficulties, emotional difficulties, and stints in rehab are played out in the media.

It's important to remember that the media shows us, not what is ordinary, but what is out of the ordinary. News reports, celebrity shows and magazines, and "reality" TV thrive on the exciting, the lurid, and the bizarre. The many wealthy people who live undramatic, productive, and useful lives don't get any more media attention than anyone else.

After working with many families, my view is that dysfunctional and destructive behaviors aren't specific to wealthy families but are part of our larger culture. Families from all walks of life and all income levels face challenges like addiction, depression, mental health problems, family conflicts, power struggles, and overspending. In wealthy families, those challenges just play out on a larger stage.

While money itself is neutral, however, wealth does serve as an accelerant. No matter what people are like, if you add money, they'll be more that way. Someone who is a spender on a modest income will become more so if you add in a few million dollars. Somewhat ironically, if someone is frugal, money will exacerbate that trait as well. If there's anxiety or depression in the family, money will foster more of it. Drinkers or drug users don't become addicts because they have money, they just become addicts who use more expensive substances.

I've discovered over the years that part of my role with families is to help them learn more about the normal patterns that develop in families. Sometimes, what a family may have considered to be dysfunction is really just the way human beings function. When families realize that many of their challenges and ways of relating to each other are normal, they find it easier to understand each other, work together, and learn more effective ways to communicate.

The coaching model I use in working with families is very much focused on looking forward and emphasizing solutions. It encourages them to ask a fundamental question: "When have we as a family been at our best?" I ask family members to talk about times they have communicated well, worked together effectively, and achieved goals that supported their mission as a family. Once they identify times when the family has been successful, we explore the factors that contributed to those successes. Then we can develop ways to build on the family's strengths in order to foster even more success in the future.

Focusing on strengths and looking toward the future, however, doesn't mean ignoring or denying difficulties in the present. Wealth may not necessarily make families more susceptible to problems like addiction, but it doesn't protect them from those problems, either. Sometimes I am asked to work with families where trust, communication, and closeness have been severely damaged. Solutions-based coaching may not be enough to help these families rebuild. It may need to be combined with other resources like education, counseling, and treatment programs.

When families face serious difficulties, an essential step toward rebuilding is to accept the reality that problems exist. It's also important to see them as family problems rather than individual problems and to understand that a great deal of help is available. Recovery is certainly possible and achievable. Indeed, when families work together, they can do more than "recover." They can restore damaged trust and rebuild family closeness so the family can thrive and become stronger than ever.

Family Systems

Jonathan, the oldest of five kids, was the responsible big brother. By the time he was 14, his parents knew they could count on him to do what he was told, and they regularly left him in charge of his three little sisters. He got good grades and never had to be reminded to do his homework. His brother Riley, only a year younger, was just the opposite. He shirked his chores, talked back, regularly got into trouble in school, and couldn't be trusted to baby-sit because he would either tease his sisters until they cried or zone out in front of the TV and forget all about them.

In reality, both the boys were fundamentally good and perfectly normal kids. It's just that Jonathan, as the oldest, had first dibs on the "big brother" role. It was natural to encourage him to be Mom and Dad's little helper when Riley was a baby, and the pattern continued as he grew older. All of us need attention, and Jonathan got his from being the helpful, reliable good kid.

For Riley, getting attention in the same way wasn't an option. The "good kid" role in the family was already filled. It was perfectly natural, then, that Riley would move into the next open position, that of the rebellious one or "bad kid." The attention he got from his parents may not have been positive, but it was still attention.

Both Jonathan and Riley loved their sisters, teased their sisters, and were sometimes careless about doing chores and homework. Yet the family saw Jonathan through a "good kid" filter and Riley through a "bad kid" filter. This tended to encourage more behavior from each boy that matched his assigned role. It also fostered conflict between the brothers.

It's easy to see the difficulties that these perceptions and conflict could carry into adulthood. Imagine Jonathan as the CFO and Riley as the sales manager of a family business, for example. Or think of the two of them, along with their parents, serving on a family board. They would continue to play out the roles assigned to them in the family system, with no one in the family understanding why they couldn't just get along and work together.

Pioneering family therapist Virginia Satir was the first to describe a pattern of roles that are typical within a family system. She identified five styles of behavior and communication:

1. The Blamer is critical, fault-finding, and accusatory.
2. The Computer intellectualizes and doesn't show emotions.
3. The Distractor uses humor or acting out to take attention away from conflict or serious issues.
4. The Leveler communicates directly and clearly.
5. The Placatory is tentative and apologetic and tends to disappear within the family.

Dr. Claudia Black and Sharon Wegscheider-Cruse adapted Satir's roles and used them in their work with people from alcoholic families. Both of them defined the roles in terms of behavior within the family rather than communication styles.

Black described the following five roles:

1. The Responsible One is a leader and decision-maker who

may also be controlling and rigid.

2. The Acting out One is creative, rebellious, and the one who often acts out family pain and gets into trouble.

3. The People Pleaser is caring, supportive, fearful, and self-denying.

4. The Adjuster is a follower who is flexible, accommodating, and easily ignored.

5. The Mascot relieves family pain with humor and distracting behavior.

Wegscheider-Cruse described very similar roles, but she consolidated them into four and renamed them. These are widely used in the addiction and codependency fields:

1. The Family Hero is the responsible, controlling leader who is often, but not always, the oldest child.

2. The Scapegoat is the one who acts out. This is often the "problem child" whose addiction, legal difficulties, or other behavior eventually calls attention to underlying problems in the family.

3. The Lost Child is the quiet, people-pleasing, invisible one.

4. The Mascot is the distractor.

While therapists most commonly use these family roles in working with dysfunctional families, almost all families will follow these patterns to some extent. Just looking at our own families, for example, most of us can pick out a Family Hero. It might be the older brother that the other siblings look to for financial advice or the sister who organizes the family get-togethers. The roles often carry over into adulthood, and it's easy to see them acted out in many family meetings.

It's a good idea, though, to be a bit cautious about labeling people with these family roles. First, the roles may change over time. The Family Hero, for example, may get frustrated with carrying the responsibility and "resign." Or other family members may rebel against the Hero's controlling behavior and stop accepting his or her leadership. If this happens, the family is thrown out of balance until someone else takes over the vacant role. Ironically, the Scapegoat is often the one who moves into the responsible leadership role. Different family members may also take on different roles from time to time, depending on the circumstances or situations.

It's also important not to be too rigid in assigning roles to family members. It is often more useful to identify the behavior rather than labeling one person as the Scapegoat, Mascot, or whatever. "When we have a family meeting, Kay usually acts like the distractor. Or Eric gets irritated and says something inappropriate, so everybody jumps on him and he serves as the scapegoat."

Adding wealth, of course, can magnify a family's patterns. Money also has its own impact on a family system. Money is energy. That energy has an impact on the lives of kids and grandkids, and one result is a disparity between generations. For example, conservative parents invariably raise liberal kids and vice versa. If grandpa was a successful oil man, the grandkids will be environmentalists. I see patterns like these all the time in the families I work with, and it's important to be mindful of them.

Paying attention to the patterns and roles in families isn't about labeling people, excusing behavior, or blaming. Instead, it's about context. Learning how family systems work can help us understand how we relate to one another within the family. The more we can see how our particular family system works, the more we can focus on the ways in which it works well and adjust the ways in which it doesn't. Understanding the dynamics of a typical family system can help family members work through difficult times and become stronger.

In coaching families, I find that they are very concerned with focusing on individual development. They want to help each family member be his or her own person and follow his or her own dreams. And that's crucial. But it's also important to maintain a balance by understanding that that the family itself is a living organism. It's more than a group of people who happen to be related. It has its own traditions, culture, and identity. Problems such as addictions, physical or mental illnesses, and unhappy relationships don't just cause pain for individual family members. They affect the family culture. Understanding the family in this way helps its members make decisions about what is best for the family as well as for individuals. It broadens the perspective and helps build long-term success for succeeding generations.

Enabling

Ethan, in his early 30s, was a leader among his siblings and cousins who made up the third generation in a wealthy family. He became concerned about the patterns of behavior he saw in his generation. They were bright, capable young adults, but two of them were obviously alcoholics and several others were experimenting with drugs. What concerned Ethan the most, though, was the family's method of dealing with these problems—or, more accurately, not dealing with them. Some family members were ignoring the addiction and drug use, while others were actively enabling the users by giving them money and helping them avoid the consequences of their behavior.

Ethan encouraged the family to begin working with an advisor who helped them define the family mission and begin to communicate more openly. They learned about addiction, family dynamics, and codependency. One crucial change in this family was in their perception that challenges like addiction were isolated, individual problems. Instead, as Ethan said, "We figured out it wasn't 'their' problem, it was 'our' problem."

Members of this family also realized that protecting addicts from the consequences of their behavior only allowed them to continue on a self-destructive course. The family made a commitment to work together to offer "tough love." They agreed on ways to limit addicts' access to family money, set boundaries about unacceptable behavior, and support those who chose treatment and recovery. They chose to stop being what the addiction recovery field calls "enablers."

Protecting the people we care about from the painful consequences of their mistakes or misbehavior is a natural impulse, born out the love we feel for our family members and the desire we have to protect and support them. At the time, it may seem like helping. Yet in the longer term, enabling isn't loving behavior. It is not in the ultimate best interests of our loved ones, because it interferes with their opportunities to learn essential life lessons that help them grow.

I'm a big fan of allowing people to experience the natural consequences of their actions. This is an essential part of effective parenting, no matter whether a child is two or forty-two. It's also one of the hardest things for any of us to do. Bailing our kids out of trouble is a constant temptation for any parent or grandparent. Staying out of the way and allowing those we love to suffer their own consequences is never easy. In wealthy families, it can be even harder because the money and the resources to make problems go away are readily available.

Enabling is part of the pattern in any family affected by challenges like addiction or psychological disorders, but it can happen in other areas as well. A pattern that is typical in many wealthy families is enabling someone's overspending. This is one kind of problem behavior where the consequences can be delayed for a long time by wealth. It takes a lot of spending before people max out their credit cards or find themselves unable to pay the bills. Sometimes spending can be a true addiction—buying as a way to deal with emotional pain. When this is the case, the spending is a serious problem, regardless of whether someone can afford it.

In other cases, overspending is more of a habit that the whole family has learned. This was the case for the Sullivan family. The parents, Paul and Connie, owned a business that had made them quite wealthy. They came to me because they were concerned about what they called "Mom and Dad's open line of credit." This family had unwittingly set up a pattern where the three kids, who were in their 30s, would come to one parent or another for help any time they needed money. There were no limits on their spending and no consequences for exceeding their income. If Dad said no, they would go to Mom. Everyone in the family had also come to assume that, if one child got something, the others needed something equivalent. A lot of back-channel communication was taking place, and everyone in the family agreed that the enabling and manipulation needed to stop.

Working with their financial planner and with me, the Sullivans set up a new system. It established some clear limits on what the parents would buy and what they wouldn't. In addition, one of the fundamental guidelines was transparency. Everyone agreed not to participate in secret money transactions. The financial advisor also volunteered to provide information on the fundamentals of budgeting and creating a financial plan and worked with me on monitoring their success in creating new patterns in the family.

A few weeks after the family retreat in which the Sullivans agreed to their new system, Paul, his two sons, and his son-in-law went to a sporting goods store to get ready for their annual fishing trip. As Paul was picking out new reels for everyone, his older son said, "Remember the new guidelines. I already spent too much on toys this month, so I can't get a new reel."

Paul's response was, "Oh, that's okay. I'll take care of it just like I always do. We just won't tell Courtney."

This man was completely sincere in wanting to change the pattern of overspending and secrecy in the family. Yet when it came down to the reality of pulling out his credit card, he slipped right back into the old pattern because that's what was familiar and comfortable.

Sabotaging our own good intentions this way is incredibly common and completely normal. In part it's due to the homeostatic principle, which is part of our basic biology. We're wired like a thermostat. It doesn't have any particular preference for 72 versus 74 or 68, but if we set it on 72, it's always going to go back to 72. If we decide we need to change and set it at 68 instead, that new temperature is uncomfortable at first and we want to go back to 72. Or, to use an example almost everyone can relate to, suppose we decide it's time to lose 20 pounds. We go out and buy some new tennis shoes and start running. The homeostatic principle is going to grab us and say, no, let's just hold on to things the way they are. As soon as we get out of breath, or our knees start to ache, or we wake up stiff and sore the next morning, we interpret that as a message telling us this running business is a bad idea. The homeostatic principle is pushing us to leave the new shoes in the closet and go back to the couch.

It's that principle that helps keep us stuck. It was part of the reason Paul automatically went back to his enabling behavior. In addition, he was driven by his unconscious emotions about money. He enjoyed being able to buy things for his kids. It felt good. It was a way of showing that he loved them.

The way we helped the Sullivans succeed in changing their behavior, first of all, was to honor the generous, loving impulse behind their financial enabling. Then we helped them focus that loving intention on the larger satisfaction and long-term goal of doing what would help the kids thrive rather than on what felt good in the moment. We helped them build a new habit of not just reacting to the immediate crisis or impulse. Instead, they learned to stop and ask, "What is the best thing to do that's in the long-term best interests of this person?"

Putting an end to enabling and replacing it with new,

healthier patterns takes time and practice, but it's well worth the effort. When family members reframe their behavior to support what I call "a purpose larger than the habit," it helps the whole family thrive.

Creating a New Emotional Legacy

Each family has an emotional legacy. It is the mood or mindset that has become embedded in the family culture over the years, often by default. Just as you can see a history of heart disease in a family for generations, you can also see a history of emotional disease or difficulty like alcoholism or narcissism. It is almost as if it's in the DNA of a family. Often this emotional legacy isn't defined; it just is. Yet when asked, family members will describe a pattern such as three generations of angry men.

I was once asked to do mediation with a family that had been involved in suing each other for three generations. I was at a disadvantage because I didn't have a history with the family, nor is mediation something that I typically do. In this case, I did so as a favor to a colleague. I interviewed each member of the family in the three generations and was surprised to find that I liked all of them. They were humble, bright, and caring people with solid Midwestern values. So where did all of the animosity come from?

What I heard about was the great-grandfather who was the wealth creator. He had many talents, but he could be mean. All of his kids were affected, with his oldest son getting the worst of the anger. This son, like his father, had many positive traits. Still, having learned from his angry father, he went on to become the same type of father to his own son. This anger and resentment was a thread in the entire family.

Over the years members of the family had learned to "settle" their differences in court. This adversarial process, with its judgments creating winners and losers, only strengthened the emotional legacy of anger.

As I prepared for the mediation with generations three and four, they had just finalized another in a series of court injunctions. I walked into the meeting unsure of the outcome but clear in my mind that these were good people caught in a negative emotional legacy. I began the meeting by telling them this. Then I asked them to provide a list detailing the characteristics of their negative family legacy. They listed anger, abuse, neglect, mistrust, and miscommunication. They began openly discussing the impact on the family for generations. The toll was significant.

I then asked them what they would like their positive emotional legacy to be for themselves and their children and grandchildren. They listed love, respect, harmony, and healthy communication. The rest of the meeting was focused on what it would take to create that desired outcome. Obviously, changing their painful emotional legacy wasn't going to happen overnight. Healing might require counseling, support, and commitment to change over a period of months or even years. But that first meeting was essential. They needed to have the pattern named so they could break free from it.

Many families, affluent or not, have unintended negative emotional legacies. Ideally, these can be identified and changed so the next generations don't have to carry the burden of those legacies. One way for families to thrive is to create a positive emotional legacy by design instead of continuing an unintended negative one.

Resources for Rebuilding Families

As a family coach, my work is to start where families are in the present and help guide them to where they want to be. I don't serve as a family therapist or a counselor for individual family members. For those who want to recover from addictions or explore deeper issues from the past, my role is to suggest resources, make referrals to therapists or treatment programs, and support the family.

In many cases, basic education about family systems and codependency is enough to help people begin to break old patterns. One important factor is that it gives them a new vocabulary and understanding. When family members learn ways to see each other as different rather than "stupid" or "wrong," they find it much easier to work together and to solve problems. There is considerable value in completing personality profiles that help people understand how they and other members of the family process information and see the world.

One simple but powerful example of the value of education concerns a middle-aged couple whose relationship was quite typical of many wealth-builder couples. The husband was a workaholic, take-charge entrepreneur and executive. His wife carried years of resentment about what she saw as his coldness or lack of love for her. I recommended that they both read *The 5 Love Languages: The Secret to Love That Lasts.* Its author, Gary D. Chapman, describes different "love languages," or types of behavior that represent giving or receiving love.

Not surprisingly, this couple discovered their primary love languages were quite different. What made her feel loved was being hugged and cuddled; what represented love to him were acts of service. No wonder, then, that when he did something like have the oil changed in her car, she didn't recognize it as a loving gesture. Learning to see each other's behavior in new ways did a great deal to bring this couple closer.

For many people, especially when addictions are involved, education and insight aren't enough to help people change their behavior. There are a great many resources available for more in-depth recovery: family therapists, individual counselors, therapeutic workshops, addiction treatment centers, and recovery support groups. Some of them are listed at the end of this book. The same family wealth that can foster enabling can also be an important resource when it comes to supporting recovery.

For families needing to rebuild and recover, the most important resource may be the sense of family identity. Each family needs to make its own choices about enabling, setting boundaries, and using family resources to help family members suffering from addictions or to address damaging patterns of behavior. My role as a family coach is to help keep the focus on the family's mission and vision and to help families decide what decisions and actions support their sense of purpose.

One of the strengths that I most admire in these families is their openness and willingness to acknowledge areas where they can use some help. Acknowledging problems and asking for help is one of the ways that thriving families foster their members' emotional and spiritual health. It is a clear sign of a family's strength and its commitment to long-term success.

CHAPTER TEN
WORKING WITH ADVISORS

"HAVING GOOD ADVISORS is like betting on the jockey rather than the horse."

"No matter how smart you are, your greatest asset is trusted advisors."

"The really successful guy is the one with enough humility to keep learning from people who know more than he does."

These quotes from members of thriving wealthy families sum up the attitude of many successful wealth builders. They are wise enough not to buy into the myth that having the skills to accumulate wealth automatically means having the skills to manage it. Working with skilled, trusted advisors is an essential part of preserving family wealth and using it well. Using advisors not only gives the family the benefit of those experts' specialized knowledge, but it also frees the family members to focus on their own unique skills and interests.

Having the humility to know what you don't know, along with the commitment to keep learning, is a characteristic I see in many of my clients. They don't behave like egotistical rock stars or out-of-control celebrities. At the same time, their humility is balanced by healthy self-confidence. The most successful wealth creators and wealth inheritors have a balanced, empowered relationship with money. They have the assurance and perspective to know what they want as individuals and as a family. They respect the skills and expertise of their advisors and are willing to learn, but they also accept that the ultimate responsibility for wealth belongs to those who own it.

Boundaries

"Never make the mistake of thinking you're a member of the family." In nearly three decades of managing the family office for a wealthy family, Lawrence routinely gave this caution to new employees when he hired them. He knew that the perks and responsibilities of working with this family, which included intimate involvement with confidential family affairs, travel on the family jet, and tickets to exclusive events, made it easy to blur the boundaries between family members and staff members.

Ultimately, though, Lawrence neglected to heed his own advice. He had originally been hired by Edgar, the second-generation family leader who had vastly expanded the wealth created by his own parents and who had established the family office. The two men worked closely together, and Lawrence was almost like another uncle to Edgar's children as they were growing up.

When Edgar died suddenly a few days before his 70th birthday, his daughter Tracy stepped into the family leadership role. Nearly 40, with a law degree and a successful career of her own, she was well qualified to deal with the family's financial affairs. Yet, to Lawrence, she was still the little girl he had given treats to or the teenager who had flunked algebra. He refused to take her seriously as the competent adult she had become. His boundaries were so rigid that he had a frozen image of Tracy and wasn't flexible enough to objectively see who she had become. He vetoed her suggestions, discounted her ideas, and "never got around to" implementing her instructions for changes in the office. Tracy tried for months to build a workable relationship with him. Finally, with great reluctance, she fired him.

Guy was the chief financial advisor for the Williams family. In a meeting with a consultant brought in by the family, his frustration erupted into a ten-minute rant. The family wealth wasn't growing. All the income was being distributed to family members or given away through the family foundation. Because of the size of the family fortune, Guy knew there was no fear of running out of money. Still, he was outraged. He believed one of the family goals should be to increase the wealth.

The consultant reminded him that "increasing the wealth" wasn't part of the Williams family's value statement. Just because Guy believed it should be a family goal didn't mean the family members felt the same way. Certainly, in Guy's role as an advisor, he had the responsibility to make sure the family members knew the wealth wasn't growing. Making decisions about whether to change the way the money was managed, however, was not up to him. Ultimately, whether the wealth was growing or not wasn't really Guy's business.

Guy's frustration and the difficulties between Lawrence and Tracy demonstrate one of the biggest challenges for both family members and advisors: boundaries. Developing the necessary close working relationship with advisors, yet still keeping clear boundaries between employers and employees, is a balancing act. It's up to both advisors and family members to maintain appropriate and workable boundaries. Keeping healthy limits in place is essential for a good working relationship that makes the best use of all the family resources.

Maintaining boundaries requires attention to the following areas:

1. Communication. Just as it is essential within the family, effective communication is key to working well with advisors. Ideally, the family governance system establishes methods of sharing information and clear lines of authority between the family and its advisors. One

sure route to chaos is for advisors to be getting conflicting instructions from multiple "bosses" without anyone knowing who is in charge. At the same time, it's important for everyone in the family to be kept fully informed and have opportunities to be heard.

Even when an effective structure to foster communication is in place, it's helpful to remember that all the communication dynamics discussed in Chapter Eight can apply to the relationships among family members and advisors as well as those within the family. This is especially true for long-term staff members who have close relationships with family members.

2. Defined Job Descriptions. No single advisor is going to have the skills and knowledge to be all things to any family. The role of an investment advisor, for example, is much different from that of a family coach. It's vital for family members and advisors to have clear definitions of each advisor's role and responsibilities.

3. Trust and Integrity. It should go without saying that a relationship of mutual trust between family members and advisors is essential. Yet that trust needs to not be given lightly, but to be earned by integrity and maintained by transparency from all parties. A system of governance and communication that fosters accountability is vital. This encourages everyone to "trust but verify" instead of blindly offering either trust or mistrust.

For advisors, maintaining clear boundaries is an important component of integrity. It's tempting, and quite normal, to want to be the go-to expert or the most trusted advisor. Yet if the advisor's need for recognition or approval becomes too important, professional integrity and ethics can begin to slip. This is when advisors become vulnerable to manipulating the people they work for, hiding mistakes, and telling employers what they want to hear instead of the truth.

Keeping a professional distance isn't the same as not having close, trusted relationships with family members. Many financial advisors are so intimately involved with the details of family members' lives that close relationships are almost inevitable. Maintaining those relationships requires everyone to be committed to full disclosure, transparency, truth-telling, and truth-hearing. It also requires everyone to remember who works for whom.

Responsibility

Defining the areas of responsibility between family members and advisors is fundamentally simple: The family decides "what" and "why." The advisors recommend "how." It's the role of family members, through a board of directors or some other system of governance, to make decisions about goals and purposes for the family resources. This goes back to the importance of having a clear statement of the family mission. Based on the family values and mission, family members decide how they want to use their financial capital as well as their broader human capital—their intellectual, social, physical, and spiritual resources. The role of advisors is to use their expertise to carry out the family's goals.

Accepting this decision-making responsibility is one of the reasons it's so important to foster leadership and wealth-management skills in later generations and to help all family members build empowered relationships with money. Those who aren't taught stewardship and responsibility may become passive recipients of the family wealth. This lack of involvement usually isn't due to a sense of entitlement or a lack of ability. Instead, it commonly stems from fear of not measuring up to previous generations, from ignorance, or from a sense that they aren't welcome or invited to be part of the decision-making process.

Welcoming younger generations into the family governance system is the responsibility of members of older generations. Advisors, however, have an important role to play as teachers and resources. This is one of the areas where Lawrence missed his opportunity to build a working relationship with Tracy. When she took over the leadership role, she would have welcomed him as a teacher and supporter had he been willing to work with her respectfully as one adult to another.

Once I received a phone call from a man who was the primary money manager for a wealthy family. He was at his wit's end because the couple who had created the wealth were over-spending so drastically. The advisor had run the numbers all sorts of ways to show them the problem. This didn't help, since the overspending was an emotional issue rather than a financial one. I told him, "You have a dilemma, and it's not your problem but the family's. You can find the best ways you can to bring it to their attention and support them in talking about it, but it's not a problem that you can fix."

I remember being at a conference for family wealth advisors, where the presenter at one session offered a case study example and asked, "What would you recommend?" All the different professionals in the room were eager to jump in and fix the problem according to their own areas of expertise. Each one, however, missed a crucial first step: finding out whether the family saw the situation as a problem. The second step would be learning what the family wanted to do. Only then would it be time for the advisors to use their skills to help create solutions.

This is one of the biggest challenges for advisors. Financial planners, therapists, and coaches understand that poor money decisions and destructive patterns around finances are not about the money. Yet in the day-to-day work of a family office, it is about the money. Taking care of the nuts and bolts of investing, filing tax returns, and paying the bills is an essential aspect of stewardship and wealth management.

Staff members in family offices live in that tension between "it's about the money" and "it's not about the money." Yet if advisors begin to care more about the money than family members do, a boundary has been crossed. Part of the balancing act for advisors is to bring their own passion and commitment to their work, but also to be clear about what is and is not their responsibility and how they can best be of service to the purposes of the family.

The Team Approach

Working with advisors may be like "betting on the jockey," but of course it's a lot more complex than that. The success of a race horse depends not only on the jockey, but also on the trainer, the owner, the exercise rider, the groom, the veterinarian, and the stable hand who cleans out the stalls. A typical wealthy family will have numerous advisors. These may include staffers in a family office, financial planners, investment advisors, accountants, financial coaches or financial therapists, attorneys, estate planners, tax planners, family coaches, and counselors.

Each of these advisors has a specific and important set of skills in his or her own field, so the challenge is to have them work together rather than having a separate bunch of experts with each one wanting to be in charge. In order for them to be effective, it's crucial that the advisors collaborate and work as a team.

This is one more reason why it's essential for family members to have confident and empowered relationships with money. It's the family that has the authority to direct the advisor team. To be effective, that direction has to be supported by a workable system of governance and communication.

The process of managing family wealth has three components:

purpose, outcome, and method. In other words: why, what, and how.

The family members, of course, are the only ones who can determine "why." Their vision of the purposes they want to achieve is what shapes all the decisions about the best uses for the family money.

Because of their training and orientation, advisors naturally tend to focus on method, the "how." Their training helps them excel at techniques, products, or deliverables. In many cases, this skill in their core competencies is exactly what families need from them.

The place where family members and advisors meet is the outcome, or "what." This is the area where they most need to work together in order to achieve the family's purposes. For advisors, particularly family planners and family coaches, this means going beyond technical skills and knowledge. It requires going a little further upstream, as it were, to access family members' key drives, motivations, and values.

A number of years ago I was attending a meeting with a family and the head of their family office. They were in the process of interviewing money managers, and on this particular day they interviewed a well-known and successful manager with a proven track record. He began the meeting with a PowerPoint presentation talking about his firm and his investment model. After about two hours, we stopped for a break. I asked the patriarch of the family about his impressions of the advisor. He gave me a stern look and said, "If he doesn't put that laptop away, I'm going to put it where the sun doesn't shine." He added, "This kid is so busy trying to impress us with his superior investment returns that he hasn't bothered to ask us anything about who we are or what we stand for."

I took the advisor aside, let him know that the client was frustrated, and gently advised him to put his laptop away and take time to get to know the family. He gave me a knowing look and then went right back to his presentation. The family didn't hire him. His choice to put method in front of purpose lost him an opportunity to manage an investment portfolio worth 50 million dollars.

My client wanted the advisor to start with understanding the family's purpose. Once the advisor knew who they were, then he could tie his sage investment advice to their purpose. Purpose acts as a touchstone. Advisors of all disciplines need to start with the unique purpose of a particular family. What is their mission? What is important to them? Once this is clear to everyone, advisors can begin the work of how best to support the results the family is looking for.

In order to foster collaboration, it's essential for advisors to learn how to communicate with each other and with the clients. One aspect of this is learning clients' communication styles and realizing that couples often have different styles. Some people "get" numbers; others don't. Financial advisors, especially those whose skills focus on the numbers, always need to be aware of the factors beyond the numbers.

One major way that advisors support families is to help them have necessary money conversations. This goes back to the disparity between the high percentage of people who believe it's important to talk with kids about money and the low percentage of people who actually do. A reluctance to be in that place of discomfort or tension is one reason we tend to procrastinate about money conversations. Advisors, being insiders in that they know details of the family's circumstances but being outsiders in that they aren't members of the family, are uniquely qualified to work within the tension. They can hold the space for family members and facilitate the money discussions that are so important. If families can't begin those conversations, their chances of creating a meaningful legacy are very slim.

The challenge and the responsibility for advisors is to excel in their core competencies, yet still work as part of an effective team. One way this comes about is for the family leaders to cultivate long-term relationships with advisors and encourage communication among the advisor team. This encourages advisors' commitment to the larger goal of being of service to this family and helping them be successful for many years.

For advisors, helping the family succeed means staying out of the way and encouraging each family to come up with its own definition of success and its own vision. It's crucial for advisors to keep their own values out of the equation. Their role is never to tell families what they should do, but to help them identify what they want to do and then give them the tools to do it. Developing the family's human capital isn't the advisor's job, but supporting the family in that development is.

In two decades, I have never seen a family come up with a bad vision. Once they have defined that vision, the role of the advisors is to support it. Their skills can help anchor the family in its purpose and use its resources to achieve what is most important to the family.

CHAPTER ELEVEN
STEWARDSHIP

"IN OUR NEXT family meeting we want to focus on steward-ship, and we'd like some information on that topic." This was the request from the Carson family to their advisor team. We came to the meeting prepared with material on stewardship—opportuni-ties for giving, methods of giving, and ideas for fostering stew-ardship as a family value. We presented our information. It fell flat. The same thing happened at a second family meeting.

At the next meeting we didn't present any material. Instead, we facilitated a conversation about what stewardship meant for this family, individually and collectively. We had learned that each family needs to define stewardship in its own way.

The idea of stewardship seems to be an integral part of a fam-ily being successful in the long term. Surprisingly, most of the families I have worked with or interviewed did not specifically list stewardship as a defined value that they were intentionally living from. Yet most of the families talked about stewardship or the essence of it as a value that they aspired to and a prac-tice that was important to them. For families who are intentional about flourishing, stewardship seems to be an essential attitude and spirit, one that isn't driven by outside expectations but that grows out of what is important to members of the family. It is part of the family's core philosophy, so fundamental that it almost goes without saying.

Defining Stewardship

Some of the families I interviewed on this topic avoided using the word "stewardship." For them, it had a religious connotation and an association with giving, usually through a church, which didn't get at the essence of what was important to them.

Yet stewardship is about more than giving. The Merriam-Webster dictionary defines it as "the careful and responsible management of something entrusted to one's care."

Seen in this sense, stewardship is about having something valuable and doing something worthwhile with it. In the case of wealth—financial and otherwise—this would mean not just preserving the wealth but increasing it and using it well. Stewardship, then, includes not just financial giving but the full and wise use of all a family's capital—intellectual, social, physical, and spiritual.

In his book *Stewardship; Lessons Learned from the Lost Culture of Wall Street*, John G. Taft says that his personal definition of stewardship evolved from the technical dictionary definition. He writes, "My new, more expansive version has to do with leaving a legacy, which I call the Golden Rule of Stewardship—*leave the world better off than you found it*—and the more existential formulation—*your purpose on earth is, ultimately, about service to others.*"

A colleague, Tim Belber, told me about one of his clients who had built a successful company and fit the stereotype of a tough-as-nails kind of guy. As they were working on his estate plan, this man told Tim he wanted his legacy to promote the gospel of Jesus Christ. He emphatically added, "I'm not talking about dogma or doctrine, but the teachings of Christ and that it is our job to be good and kind to each other." It was that spirit he wanted to see his family standing for and generating in the world.

Whether defined in religious terms or not, the theme of being of service is a common one in wealthy families. I've heard many of them use phrases like these: "We are so blessed and have been given so much, we want to give back." "We feel an obligation to leave the world a better place than we found it." "We're members of a larger community, and we need to think beyond our self-interest to how we can help others."

Most of the families I have worked with or interviewed discuss openly their sense of responsibility to be the stewards of the wealth. There is a deep sense that "to whom much is given, much is expected." In flourishing families, this sense does not come from a sense of guilt or obligation. Instead, it grows out of a sense of gratitude and a deep appreciation of how fortunate they are. They describe themselves as the custodians of their wealth and of the well-being of others.

All the families I've talked with about stewardship make clear that they aren't just speaking of financial stewardship. What matters to them is stewardship of all the gifts they have received, such as the gift of freedom and choice. One fifth-generation family—among the few that include stewardship as a stated core value—says very intentionally that "we are the stewards of our financial and spiritual resources." It is the first sentence of the family mission statement and is a commitment that each family member embodies. That commitment is obvious in the backdrop of what they invest in and their philanthropic interests.

In families like this one, you can see the stewardship in family member's connections to each other and in their investment in the community. It is an investment beyond them as individuals to a sense of legacy. They want their family to be proud stewards of their wealth. The sense of legacy becomes a part of the fabric of the family.

I have worked with a number of families who had very different political or social beliefs from each other, but they were in alignment around the value of making a contribution in the lives of others. It's common for wealthy families to want to do good things with their resources.

Creating a Legacy of Stewardship

Stewardship in families is a long-term vision, a legacy of both giving back to the larger community and helping the family flourish over many years. It is framed in terms of, "What will be best for my family years from now?" Al Watts, in his book *Navigating Integrity*, says, "Effective stewardship requires that ability to see the distant effect of our decisions and actions today—where distance may be measured in many miles or many generations."

Families that are successful have intentional conversations about stewardship. They work together to answer questions such as: "How do we use our wealth wisely and effectively?" "What does stewardship look like for us as a family?" "How do we deal with our individual differences?" These conversations can help family members change their relationship with the wealth. Really underscoring a sense of stewardship and giving back is one of the most dynamic things that can break families free from the cycle of entitlement.

A few wealthy families have attempted to create a legacy of stewardship by requiring family members who receive income from trust funds to give a certain percentage to charity. One serious drawback to this approach is that it removes much of someone's control or choices about giving. Trust fund recipients who have to justify their lifestyle and choices in order to receive their income from year to year are kept in a state that one man described to me as "living my life on probation." Forced giving is just another aspect of that dependency. It seldom fosters the sense of true stewardship that is part of an empowered relationship with wealth.

Flourishing families have found it more effective to create a sense of stewardship by example. It's important for families and their advisors to bring up the issue of stewardship, treat it as an important success factor, and undertake to discover what it means for them. This discovery often includes focused conversations about stewardship. Perhaps even more important, however, is the behavior that older generations in the family model for children and grandchildren. As with so many things, it is our actions that most clearly reveal whether our approach to life is built on a sense of service that goes deeper than just financial giving.

I remember my two teenage children balking one year as we were preparing to go to their grandparents' home to set up Christmas decorations and trim the tree. As is typical of teenagers, they were reluctant to get out of bed early to do something for someone else, even their grandparents. They asked the age-old question, "Why do we have to do this?" Even as I opened my mouth to give them the standard response of, "Because I said so," I noticed my own ambivalence about the task. It occurred to me that providing this help to the older generation was more than an obligation. It was an act of service. It was a way to honor my parents and my children's grandparents, to express our appreciation for their presence in our lives. Articulating that spirit seemed to make a significant difference to all of us. Rather than dutifully carrying boxes up and down the stairs while rolling our eyes, we all felt grateful for the opportunity to be of service.

Balancing Stewardship and Personal Passion

James E. (Jay) Hughes, author of *Family Wealth—Keeping It in the Family*, sees stewardship as only one aspect of a balanced and healthy relationship with wealth. He uses the Chinese yin/yang symbol to illustrate his view, with pursuit of a personal dream on the left and stewarding your gifts on the right. He emphasizes that the two sides should be in balance and mutually supportive of each other.

In an interview, Jay told me that, in his experience, most wealth creators spend 90% of their lives pursuing their passions and dreams. Then later in their lives their attention turns to stewarding their gifts. He went on to explain that often members of the next generation may focus on stewardship to such an extent that they fail to pursue their own dreams. They feel such a responsibility to take care of the family legacy that they lose sight of their own needs. The classic example comes to mind of children who grow up in a family business with the expectation that working in the business is their only career option, which deprives them of pursuing their own dream and passion.

Jay also made the compelling statement that financial advisors to wealthy families tend to over-emphasize stewardship. Our focus instead should be on helping families create balance by encouraging the individual dreams and passions of the next generation. He points out that asking the next generation to carry the mantle of being stewards before they have a chance to focus on their own fulfillment defies the normal individuation process. Indeed, most developmental models describe maturation as the ability to differentiate from our early attachments and form an identity of our own separate from our family of origin.

A primary wish for most parents is to have healthy and happy children. In many of my interviews, parents spoke with pride of their children's various accomplishments, from the schools they attended to their involvement in the family business. Yet most of them returned to the basics that all parents can relate to—my wish is for my children to be happy as individuals and with their choices in life.

Research shows that one element of happiness is a sense of gratitude. In his book *Thanks!: How the New Science of Gratitude Can Make You Happier*, Robert Emmons states that we have a happiness set point. This explains why the joy of purchasing something like a new car wears off about the same time as the new car smell. Our ego has us believe that a new house or new relationship or new shoes will make us happier, but in reality, regardless of what we acquire, our perception of happiness returns to our original set point. Yet his research found that gratitude does affect our perception of happiness. He found that gratitude is natural for some, but for most of us it is something we need to practice. Those who keep a gratitude journal or who start or end their day reciting what they are grateful for show increased levels of happiness.

Researchers Adam Grant and Jane Dutton took this a step further. Their work demonstrated that thinking about times when we have given to others is more effective in promoting generosity than being grateful. Thinking about times that we have given or been of service to others motivates us to be more generous.

Fostering a sense of gratitude, then, is an essential role for families who want to create a legacy of both stewardship and individual happiness. The image of stewardship and individual development being in flow or a dynamic looking for balance is a powerful one for both advisors and family members to keep in mind. It may help families to remember to ask and answer the following questions: Are we truly encouraging the young adults to pursue their dreams instead of ours? Are we supporting the elder generations in exploring a deep sense of stewardship for them and their family? Are we engaging in the power of conversation to define what stewardship means for us as well as what it will look like to be of service?

Another colleague I interviewed, Barb Culver, described stewardship as a developmental journey. Her view is that stewardship emerges after other concerns are addressed: creating the wealth, preserving and sustaining the wealth, and dealing with the lessons of how much is enough. Stewardship, like financial literacy, often needs to be taught, and the teaching is accepted if it connects with a general attitude or acceptance of stewardship.

Barb compared stewardship to Maslow's hierarchy of needs, which describes human psychological development as progressing through stages from basic survival to emotional and spiritual fulfillment. The needs are described as Physiological, Safety,

Love/Belonging, Esteem, and Self-Actualization. In a similar way, the evolution of stewardship follows a pattern of Earning, Sustaining, Enriching, Legacy, and Stewardship.

This comparison fits with the pattern I've observed in many of my client families. While it is important to model the spirit of service and stewardship, active stewardship is primarily the path of the senior generation. It is consistent with their development to be generative, to create a lasting legacy that includes encouraging the future generations to find their own dreams. Ultimately it is the job of all members of each generation to first forge their own identities separate from the family. Then, as they are able to develop their own set of muscles, they will be able to return to the family and better be able to support a lasting legacy.

Seen in this way, active stewardship is a part of the normal life stages for each generation. The role of the family is not to impose or require stewardship, but to foster both the pursuit of individual passions and the value of giving back to the community.

Teaching stewardship to younger generations, then, includes encouraging them to see themselves as capable stewards of their own intellectual and emotional capital as well as the family's financial capital. Supporting individual development— as opposed to individual gratification—is a powerful way for families to build an attitude of appreciation. It encourages family members to be grateful for the blessing and gift of the family wealth and to value themselves and their own separate gifts as well. Flourishing families encourage individuals to see themselves as worthy of the wealth, not in the sense of "having money makes me better than other people," but in the sense of "I am capable of using this gift well."

Individual family members who are encouraged to follow their dreams will tend to focus on personal success in the earlier stages of their lives. As they grow older, this self-fulfillment and emotional richness builds a sense of gratitude and appreciation that evolves into giving back in satisfying ways. Stewardship seems to be the central theme that ties together the legacy of purpose, meaning, and fulfillment that most of us hope for in our children.

CHAPTER TWELVE
Intentional Wealth

OVER MY YEARS as a consultant and coach, I've consulted with many wealthy families and interviewed many others. They've had a variety of lifestyles, cultures, systems, and values. I've met families adapting to newly created wealth, families with several generations of inherited wealth, families struggling with patterns of addiction and codependency, families torn by conflict, and families that were doing well and wanted to do even better.

There's just one kind of family I've never encountered: a "bad" one. To paraphrase Will Rogers, I've never met a family I didn't like. Even those in the midst of serious difficulties are well-intentioned, likeable, good people. These families have one thing in common: they want their children and grandchildren to succeed. They want to leave a legacy of health, balance, and empowerment.

They already have the most important component of success, the intention to succeed. All they need is some tools to help transform that intention into reality. One of the most important things I've learned in my years of working with families is that families don't flourish by accident. Families that create legacies of success and stewardship do so intentionally.

The Hero's Journey

*"Your time is limited, so don't waste it living someone else's
life. Don't be trapped by dogma—which is living with the
results of other people's thinking. Don't let the noise of
other's opinions drown out your own inner voice. And most
important, have the courage to follow your heart and intuition.
They somehow already know what you truly want to become.
Everything else is secondary."*

Steve Jobs

Following our heart and our intuition is what takes each of us on
our own "hero's journey." Author Joseph Campbell wrote about
this concept in books like *The Hero with a Thousand Faces.*

Mythology is filled with stories of heroes who undertake
journeys where they overcome obstacles, challenges, and terrors
to achieve a great purpose. Along the way they discover inner
strength and abilities they never knew they had. This archetype
is repeated over and over, from ancient literature to modern stories like *Lord of the Rings* and *Star Wars.*

It's easy to see the hero's journey in terms of adventures taking place far, far away, featuring characters that are larger than
life. Yet this myth can also be seen as an analogy for a journey
each of us needs to make. This journey applies equally to everyone, no matter what our gender, our family circumstances, our
social or financial status, or our career choices. It is an exploration, an endeavor to find our own voice, purpose, and passion.
Each of us needs to undertake that journey in our own way and
follow our own path in our own direction. It is truly the journey
of a lifetime, unique to each person.

To put it even more simply, the hero's journey is the process
of growing into maturity. We travel through the years, encoun-
tering difficulties along the way, learning to know ourselves and
use our strengths, and ultimately achieving wisdom. We learn

who we are, become confident in our own abilities, and become independent individuals.

The journey toward maturity might be seen as a circle. In the beginning, as children, we are protected by our parents and families. At some point, it is important for us to separate from the family in order to follow our dreams and become our true selves. In doing so, we take some of the family's values and strengths with us. Ideally, those values will support us in creating our separate identities. Once we have learned to be independent and have gained maturity, we come back into the family in a new way. We bring our strengths as whole, unique individuals into the family culture and make it even stronger.

In families that flourish, the children and grandchildren are encouraged and supported in going through these normal life stages in healthy ways. The role of the family is to encourage younger generations to grow up and become whole, rather than allowing the wealth to foster immaturity and dependence.

One of the most essential roles for parents and grandparents in this process is to allow and encourage children to make their own hero's journeys. This is a challenge for any of us as parents, because what we want to do is to smooth the way for our children and protect them from pain.

This protective impulse is one of the obstacles that lie in the way of the hero's journey for anyone. It can especially be a challenge for members of later generations in wealthy families. Not only do these parents want to protect their children from hardship, as we all do, but in many cases they have the financial means to do it. It's hard to make a hero's journey when someone is trying to take care of you by buying off all the dragons and paving the road from beginning to end. Turning the hero's journey into a luxury excursion takes away the travelers' opportunity to find those inner qualities that are so essential for maturity, life satisfaction, and happiness.

Another obstacle for many members of wealthy families is

the tendency to mythologize the original creators of the family wealth. Later generations often see them as larger-than-life heroes who have overcome hardships to achieve great things. It's easy to look back and see the heroes' journeys that these wealth creators have made. It can be much more difficult for their descendants to see either the necessity for or the possibilities in heroes' journeys of their own. For one thing, their lives may be comfortable and relatively free from external hardships. In addition, they may compare themselves to their hard-driving ancestors and feel as if they can't measure up to that impossible standard.

Yet because the hero's journey is primarily an inner, emotional one, making it is just as essential for someone from a wealthy family as for someone who struggles to overcome financial deprivation. For wealth inheritors, one aspect of the hero's journey may be to get past the superficial label of "rich" to become who they are as individuals. For any of us, this journey is the process of understanding who we are and then finding the courage to do what we need to do in order to follow our passion and purpose. Finding that courage may well be the hardest part. For one thing, undertaking a hero's journey means leaving behind what is comfortable and familiar, which is never easy. In wealthy families, there is often a strong set of assumptions and expectations about "what it means to be part of this family." The expectations that are part of the family culture can be confining, and breaking away from them requires strength and bravery.

The introduction to *The Power of Myth,* by Joseph Campbell and Bill Moyers, includes this statement about the hero's journey: "Campbell said, '… The ultimate aim of the quest must be neither release nor ecstasy for oneself, but the wisdom and the power to serve others.' One of the many distinctions between the celebrity and the hero, he said, is that one lives only for self while the other acts to redeem society."

Maybe "redeeming society" is a little too much to expect

of ourselves as ordinary individuals making our own ordinary heroes' journeys. Yet if we think instead in terms of "contributing to society," that's a responsibility each of us can accept in our own ways. It certainly describes the attitude of stewardship and gratitude that I see in so many flourishing families. What I hear, in various ways, from families I work with is a value of wanting to help members of later generations follow their passions and dreams in ways that contribute to society rather than merely satisfying their own desires. These families want to use their wealth to support family members in being their best selves and defining themselves in ways that aren't about the money. As families, they don't want to foster celebrities, they want to foster heroes.

The Presence Triangle

In earlier chapters I've discussed that the internal culture and values of a family aren't necessarily the same as the external perceptions that outsiders may have of the family. Yet the family's culture and values shape the way that family and its individual members present themselves to the larger world. Creating a healthy family culture starts with the Presence of its individual members.

Presence is the way we are in the world. It is our sense of who we are, as expressed through connection, purpose, and contribution. One way to think of Presence is as a reminder that each of us is a "human being," not a "human doing." It is about being present in what we're doing, participating fully, and being in the moment.

A phrase that's sometimes used in business coaching is "leadership presence" or "executive presence." I've seen companies spend lots of time and money "polishing" executives. The effort often focuses on externals like becoming fluent speakers, having the right clothes, and in other ways presenting the right image. This is a waste of time. What people need and want from leaders, in both businesses and families, is presence in a real way. Speaking and acting from an authentic sense of purpose and connection, being our genuine selves in all situations, is what makes up a true leadership presence. This is the kind of presence that we respond to and respect.

Three factors that affect the way we present ourselves to others are Cognition, Body, and Mood.

Cognition is balance in our thinking. It is a willingness to weigh information and to suspend judgment of both ourselves and others. We might describe this as a willingness to set aside the emotional baggage that can cloud our perception. Our thinking is clear and focused, not polluted by the "shoulds" of life.

Body is how we are physically present in a given situation. It includes the signals we send with our body language, such as leaning into a conversation or pulling back from it. Body also includes our physical well-being, which is why taking care of our basic needs is so important. It is being balanced in how we approach our life in any given situation.

Mood is something deeper than, say, a superficial attitude of annoyance because we got caught in traffic on our way to a meeting. It is a deeper mindset that is part of who we are. A greatly over-simplified description of mood is our basic sense of either possibility/optimism or despair/pessimism. A balanced mood is that of acceptance—accepting in the moment both who we are and who others are.

I find it useful to think of cognition, body, and mood as constituting a wheel. As long as these aspects are in balance so the wheel is round, our mood is in balance. If we feel out of balance, focusing on one of these aspects will move us in the right direction. For example, if you are feeling stuck and depressed, challenging your negative thoughts can have a positive effect on your mood. Or going for a brisk walk or bike ride can shift a negative mood. Some of the things I've discussed in previous chapters, like gratitude and appreciation, are ways to shift our moods.

Businesses have moods, and so do families. For example, a family's mood might be supportive or competitive. I recently worked with a family that was highly competitive. Each member was successful in his or her own right, and each was involved in competitive sports. You could feel the mood of competition and distrust. This family identified mistrust of each other as the primary barrier to their success. As they began to create experiences of cooperation within the family, the mood began to switch from dog-eat-dog competition to, "How can we win together?"

One aim of family coaching is to identify the family mood and help shift it toward gratitude and stewardship rather than entitlement. In working with families, I often illustrate this with a model that I call the Presence Triangle.

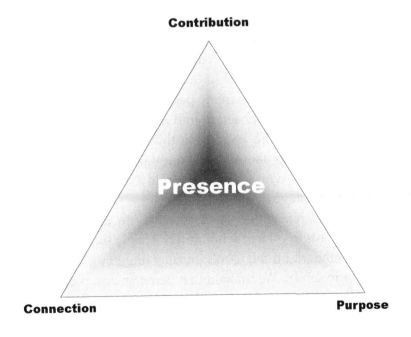

Connection. As human beings, we have a fundamental drive for connection. We need to connect both with ourselves and with other people. A lot of the coaching I do with families and individuals is about developing that essential connection with ourselves, learning to know and be comfortable with who we are. Yet we also need connections with others in healthy ways. Each of us—even introverts and those who thrive in solitude—needs to be heard. It's important for us to be in relationships that offer reciprocity, where giving and taking go both ways.

We long for that deeper sense of connection with others. We also long for a spiritual connection. This isn't necessarily within a specific religious context, but is a longing to connect to spirit. It is a need for the sense of oneness and the awareness that we're all connected.

Before we can have an authentic connection with another person, we first need to be connected with ourselves. Most of our young adulthood is about finding a partner, establishing a career path, and starting a family. It many respects it is very externally focused, as we try on various roles in an attempt to identify who we are. Many adults become disillusioned as they realize that a particular career or relationship doesn't give them the meaning they were hoping for. How many people do we know who have uttered the phrase, "I just need to find myself." It is an honest cry.

For many of us, the awareness that we are not connected with ourselves brings about a dark night of the soul. It's painful to realize, "I'm not who I have been told I am. I'm not the role that I have been playing."

This painful realization opens the way to the next and all-important question: "Then who am I?" This is the question that leads us to embark on the hero's journey of getting connected to our authentic selves. We make much better mates, parents, family members, colleagues, and participants in our communities if we have initiated that particular journey.

Purpose. This is our primary drive to have a fulfilling life.

Purpose describes who each person is at a deep level. It is about who we are essentially. Every person's purpose is different, but we each have a fundamental purpose. We may need help to identify that purpose and learn what it will take to be a purposeful human being and how to be purposeful in our daily lives. When we are living our lives from purpose, we use our passion as a guide rather than being governed by "shoulds."

One middle-aged man I interviewed for this book was Miles, a member of the fourth generation in a successful wealthy family. His story was about finding purpose in his life. Initially, his life went according to the script. He graduated from college with honors, immediately went off to law school, and started working in the family office as soon as he received his law degree. Within five years he was running the family office and by all reports doing an exceptional job.

By this time Miles was married with two young children. As he described it, he was leading a charmed life, right on track. That is, until he was diagnosed with a virulent form of cancer that threatened his life. He openly talked about how the cancer almost consumed him and, as he faced death, what was most prominent in his mind was regret. He remembered that from a young age his dream had been to be a teacher, and that somewhere along the way he just ended up with a business and law degree instead. He spoke about feeling as if he were on automatic pilot in his career. He never planned on running the family office; it just seemed to happen.

It became clear to Miles that somewhere along the way he had lost his dream. He vowed that if he made it through the cancer, he would pick up that lost dream.

Miles did recover, and he did go back to his initial purpose. If this were a movie, that's probably where it would end, with tears of joy and uplifting music. But Miles was clear that his was not a Disney story and not that simple. Initially his family questioned his decision. Some of his friends thought that leaving a lucrative position to be a school teacher was an impulsive, emotional decision and not an intelligent move. But slowly, friends and family members began to see that for Miles it was truly about following his purpose.

When I spoke to him, Miles was a high school teacher. Even though he had left the family office, he was still involved with his family and had found a new way to contribute to it by heading up the family council. He joked about how little he was making financially, but he also reported that he truly felt blessed. He even felt fortunate in a way to have had the cancer, because it ultimately gave him his freedom.

For many of us, purpose in life is replaced with obligations. We need to honor that which is within us and allow purpose to be the touchstone from which we make the decisions that guide our future.

Contribution. This is what we do, how we each fulfill our purpose. It isn't enough merely to focus on our inner development and discover our purpose. Making a difference and a contribution requires us to take action to fulfill that purpose. Taking action requires courage and effort, and it is where strategies like goal-setting come in. Our contribution is how we manifest our purpose in the world.

I worked with a young couple from Silicon Valley who had invented a really cool technology that made them a lot of money in their late 20s. They were delightful people who were literally living the dream. Yet they started working with me in their 30s because they felt stuck.

They had a great life but had this nagging feeling that they wanted to make a contribution of some kind. Yet they weren't sure where and how. After doing some shared values and visioning work, the husband blurted out, "The answer is water. Lack of a clean water supply is a significant issue for many people. How can we research and learn more about what is being done? How can we use our technology and research skills to really make a difference in this area where there is so much need?"

Given a need on which to focus that suited their interests and skills, that passion for making a difference became their North Star.

We all have a version of "I want to make a contribution to my family, community, or world." Using the Presence Triangle is one way to help clarify that vision and provide clearer answers to the question, "What will be my contribution?"

It's Not About the Money

As we were preparing for a family meeting, the head of one family told me, "It needs to be 20% about money and 80% about following their dreams."

One of the most important benefits of building a healthy, empowered relationship with money is gaining the freedom to understand that life isn't about the money. Certainly, the money is important. The thriving families that I see have a strong sense of gratitude for the benefits and privileges that wealth provides. They appreciate that the foundation of security and choice it establishes allows them to focus on the emotional side—relationships, career satisfaction, fulfillment, and stewardship.

When in family meetings I facilitate "talking circles" about success, these families don't focus on investments or assets or increasing their financial net worth. They focus on the less tangible Family Net Worth that consists of the family's entire human and intellectual capital. They talk about things like character, values, passions, and dreams. They understand that success is not about what they have, but about what they do and who they are, as individuals and as families.

Going from "shirt sleeves to success" is no accident. It doesn't just happen because some families are luckier than others; it's possible for any family. Families that flourish do so because they manage the family's financial and non-financial resources with attention and intention. This kind of success means much more than maintaining the family's financial legacy or enjoying prosperity. It means passing on purposeful legacies of value, empowerment, family connection, and stewardship. When families make a commitment to intentional wealth, they create a legacy of wealth that is enhanced by but not limited to financial success. They build a heritage that fosters rich and fulfilling lives for generations to come.

ABOUT THE AUTHOR

COURTNEY PULLEN, MA, is the President of the Pullen Consulting Group, a Denver-based firm that provides services in management consulting, business coaching, family wealth counseling, leadership development, and communication.

Courtney received his graduate degree in Psychology from the University of Northern Colorado in 1983. He taught at both the University of Denver and the University of Colorado at Denver. He has served clients for more than 25 years, first as a psychotherapist and currently as a coach and consultant for professional services firms and wealthy families.

A Professional Certified Coach, Courtney is a graduate of the Newfield coaching program. He has conducted numerous workshops and presentations in the areas of individual and organization change, behavioral finance, and family wealth counseling. He is a former contributing editor to the *Journal of Financial Planning* and *Journal of Practical Estate Planning* as well as a faculty member of the Sudden Money Institute.

RESOURCES

Books

The Anatomy of Peace: Resolving the Heart of Conflict, the Arbinger Institute (Berrett-Koehler Publishers, 2008)

Appreciative Inquiry: A Positive Revolution in Change, David L. Cooperrider and Diana Whitney (Berrett-Koehler Publishers, 2005)

Authentic Happiness: Using the New Positive Psychology to Realize Your Potential for Lasting Fulfillment, Martin E. P. Seligman (Atria Books, 2004)

Beyond Gold; True Wealth for Inheritors, Thayer Cheatham Willis (New Concord Press, 2012)

Callings: Finding and Following an Authentic Life, Gregg Levoy (Three Rivers Press, 1997)

Change Your Questions, Change Your Life: 10 Powerful Tools for Life and Work, Marilee Adams, PhD (Berrett-Koehler Publishers, Second Edition, 2009)

The Communication Catalyst, Mickey Connolly and Richard Rianoshek (Kaplan Publishing, 2001)

The Cycle of the Gift: Family Wealth and Wisdom, James E. Hughes Jr., Susan E. Massenzio, and Keith Whitaker (Bloomberg Press, 2013)

Difficult Conversations: How to Discuss What Matters Most, Douglas Stone, Bruce Patton, and Sheila Heen (Penguin Books, Revised Edition, 2010)

Family Wealth—Keeping It in the Family: How Family Members and Their Advisers Preserve Human, Intellectual, and Financial Assets for Generations, James E. Hughes, Jr. (Bloomberg Press, 2004)

The 5 Love Languages: The Secret to Love That Lasts, Gary D. Chapman (Northfield Publishing, 2009)

The Hero with a Thousand Faces, Joseph Campbell (New World Library, Third edition, 2008)

The Inheritor's Sherpa; A Life-Summiting Guide for Inheritors by Myra Salzer (The Wealth Conservancy, Inc., 2005)

Mastery: The Keys to Success and Long-Term Fulfillment, George Leonard (Plume, 1992)

Money and Meaning: New Ways to Have Conversations About Money with Your Clients, Judith Stern Peck (Wiley, 2007)

Money Harmony, Olivia Mellan (Walker & Company, 1995)

Navigating Integrity, Al Watts (Brio Press, 2011)

The Power of Myth, Joseph Campbell and Bill Moyers (Anchor, 1991)

Presence: Human Purpose and the Field of the Future, Peter M. Senge, C. Otto Scharmer, Joseph Jaworski, and Betty Sue Flowers (The Society for Organizational Learning, 2004)

The Price of Privilege: How Parental Pressure and Material Advantage Are Creating a Generation of Disconnected and Unhappy Kids, Madeline Levine, Ph.D. (HarperCollins, 2006)

Pygmalion in the Classroom: Teacher Expectation and Pupils' Intellectual Development, Robert Rosenthal and Lenore Jacobson (Irvington Publishers, 1992)

Raising Financially Fit Kids, Joline Godfrey (Ten Speed Press; Revised Edition, 2013)

Stewardship: Lessons Learned from the Lost Culture of Wall Street, John G. Taft, Charles D. Ellis, John C. Bogle (Wiley, 2012)

Sudden Money: Managing a Financial Windfall, Susan Bradley and Mary Martin (Wiley, 2000)

Thanks!: How the New Science of Gratitude Can Make You Happier, Robert Emmons (Houghton Mifflin Harcourt, 2007)

The 3 Big Questions for a Frantic Family, Patrick Lencioni (Jossey-Bass, 2008)

Transitions: Making Sense of Life's Changes, William Bridges (Da Capo Press; Second Edition, 2004)

20 Secrets to Money and Independence: A Guide to Independence, Economic Empowerment, and Self-Awareness, Joline Godfrey (St. Martin's Press, 2000)

Wealth in Families, Charles W. Collier (Harvard University Press, Third Edition 2012)

A Wealth of Possibilities: Navigating Family, Money, and Legacy, Ellen Miley Perry (Egremont Press, 2012)

Wired for Wealth, Brad Klontz, Ted Klontz, and Rick Kahler (HCI, 2008)

You are What You Say: The Proven Program that Uses the Power of Language to Combat Stress, Anger, and Depression, Mathew Budd and Larry Rothstein (Harmony, 2001)

12-Step Programs

Alcoholics Anonymous
www.aa.org

Al-Anon/Alateen for family members and friends of alcoholics
www.al-anon.alateen.org

Narcotics Anonymous
www.na.org

Made in the USA
Middletown, DE
02 March 2022